THE
DREAM CYCLE

THE
DREAM CYCLE

*Leveraging the Power
of Personal Growth*

Steve Moore

wesleyan
publishing
house

Indianapolis, Indiana

Copyright © 2004 by Steve Moore
Published by Wesleyan Publishing House
Indianapolis, Indiana 46250
Printed in the United States of America

ISBN 0-89827-277-7

Library of Congress Cataloging-in-Publication Data

Moore, Steve, 1960-
  The dream cycle : leveraging the power of personal growth / Steve Moore.
    p. cm.
  ISBN 0-89827-277-7 (hardcover)
  1. Success—Religious aspects—Christianity. I. Title.
  BV4598.3.M66 2004
  248.4—dc22
                                    2003027843

To my dad, the ultimate dreamer-leader in my life: thanks for modeling a passion-filled life of learning and growing. To my mom, the ultimate dream-nurturer: thanks for keeping God's dreams for me alive, in the darkest of nights, before I knew how to dream for myself.

To my wife, Sherry: thanks for helping me grow and for dreaming with me. To my children, Alaina, Ashley, Alison and Josiah: may you be true to your God-inspired dreams.

Contents

Preface

E very one of us is on a journey toward who we want to be, who we were meant to be, and what we will achieve with our lives. Making progress on that dream-inspired journey will require us to grow. The subject of personal growth is not just for leaders or overachievers; it is for everyone. That means this book is for you, regardless of your leadership aptitude or your stage in life. The fact that you even picked up this book is an indication that a dreamer lives inside of you. If this book came to you as a gift, someone saw in you a potentially influential person, someone worth his or her investment. As you continue reading, you will find yourself among friends.

What I Know about You

My guess is that you could look back at the last twelve months of your life and quickly identify some evidence of growth. Also, you would probably admit that the rate and extent of your growth could have been greater—and that you wish they had been. You've grown, but not as much as you'd like. Am I right so far?

Here's what else I know: next year will be different. In the following twelve months, you will take giant steps toward becoming the person you want to be and achieving the things you most want to do with your life.

How do I know that?

Imagine two identical trees planted side by side. They are the same age, the same species, and are planted in the same climate, but one gets fertilized and the other doesn't. You tell me what will happen. Obviously, the tree that gets fed will grow while the tree that is starved for nourishment will languish. Now think of the two trees as two successive years in your life and imagine that this book is a good load of fertilizer. No, I'm not saying the book is a lot of compost! If it were, I'd give it to a tree. But I do believe this book will do for you what fertilizer would do for a tree—stimulate growth. So please grow with me through the three adventures that comprise this journey.

- The Power of Dreaming

- The Power of Growing

- The Power of Multiplying

WHAT YOU NEED TO KNOW ABOUT ME

Helping people realize their dreams is my passion. My work involves developing leaders in both the non-profit and corporate sectors, touching the church and the market place. I have worked extensively with young leaders through relationships with Emerging Young Leaders, Top Flight Leadership, and Growing Leaders, organizations that focus on emerging Christian leaders, from middle schoolers to young adults. A new organization, Keep Growing Inc., provides me the opportunity to work with established leaders in a wide range of settings. For more than fifteen years, I've been helping people realize their dreams by leveraging the power of personal growth.

There's something else you should know about me: I'm a person who has a profound faith in the God of the Bible, which serves as both a filter and an anchor for all of my life. The convictions that result from my faith have given me a perspective that colors the ideas I will share with you. The spiritual concepts and biblical examples in this book are a reflection of my beliefs. But the subject of personal growth is not confined to those who share my faith journey. The principles I relate in this book will aid in your personal development, regardless of your faith perspective. My aim is to help you become the person you dream of being—especially if your dream adds value to others.

I'd love to hear from you twelve months from now, and maybe I will. Whatever your dream is—even if it hasn't yet poked its head through the floor of your consciousness—I'm confident you will be much closer to its realization when we conclude this journey a few pages from here. Who knows? we may even end up working on the same dream!

So instead of offering you a Jiminy Cricket wish that your dreams will all come true, let me offer a far more meaningful prayer: may you be true to your dream.

WITH THANKS

The ultimate test of an idea is whether or not it will work. I knew the ideas in this book worked for me, but the real question was whether they would work for others. I want to thank Jeff Galley, Stephen Blandino, Jeof Oyster, Cheryl Pfautz, and Allison Barnes for giving me a real-life laboratory to apply the Dream Cycle in an organizational context. Your application of these principles and subsequent personal development have confirmed that these ideas *really do* work and have given me the confidence to share them with a wider audience.

Thanks also to Steve Gardner; your counsel, insight and editorial genius raised this entire project to a new level. I love working with you.

Finally, I want to thank two people at Wesleyan Publishing House: Don Cady and Larry Wilson. Thanks, Don, for seeing potential in me and in this project. Thanks, Larry, for challenging me not to settle for anything but my best.

For those who join me on this dream-laced journey, I have one simple exhortation: keep growing!

STEVE MOORE

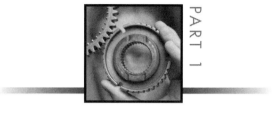

PART 1

The Power of Dreaming

You have the power to realize your dreams.

God-inspired dreams are not placed in your heart as a taunt.
If your dream is truly God given, you can reach it.

ONE

Personal Capacity

The Power to Realize Your Dreams

No one knows how close we can come to realizing 100 percent of our potential. You may have heard it said that most people use only 10 percent of their mental capacity. Although that may be true, there is no scientific data to support such a claim. Actually, that notion can be traced to a casual observation made by Albert Einstein. Since many of his scientific theories proved true, the 10 percent figure has been widely accepted—perhaps to Einstein's amusement.

Psychological researchers have measured the total mental, or psychic, energy available in a life span of seventy-five years. The term *psychic energy,* in this context, refers to thinking power, not mental telepathy or other paranormal abilities. Experts figure that the brain processes about 110 bits of information per second. To put that in perspective, it requires about forty bits to understand what another person is saying. This means that over a period of seventy-five years, deducting an average of eight hours sleep time per day, a human being has the capacity to process some 173 *billion* bits of information.[1]

While 173 billion bits sounds like an astoundingly large volume of information, remember that much of our mental energy is expended in the most mundane routines of life—getting ready for work, deciding what to eat for breakfast, and making the daily commute. The sobering reality is that every conscious moment of our lives must be accounted for in terms of mental energy, and every conversation, thought, or feeling expends some of this limited and precious resource.

This begs a worthwhile question: on what are you spending your psychic capital? Are you wasting it on thoughts and activities that do not produce lasting memories, refine ideas, develop new skills, or strengthen relationships? Or are you investing your mental energy in activities that sharpen your skills, expand your understanding of a subject, or deepen relationships? This kind of expenditure generates a return in the form of an improved quality of life in the future. In other words, it helps you grow.

When we think of mental capacity in those terms, the operative question is not how much capacity do most human beings use, but how much do *you* use? How are you spending your mental energy, and what are you getting in return?

THE CAPACITY INDEX

A simple way to measure your use of mental energy is by using a diagram I call the *Capacity Index*. Here's how it works: draw a vertical line on a piece of paper, or even in the margin of this page. At the top of the line, write "100 Percent." At the bottom of the line, write "0 Percent." Now place a horizontal mark at the top of the line (at the 100 percent level) and label it "P," which stands for your *potential*. This represents your maximum capacity—100 percent of your physical, mental, social, and spiritual potential.

Now place a second horizontal mark at whatever point on this line represents your present level of development. Label this mark "A," which

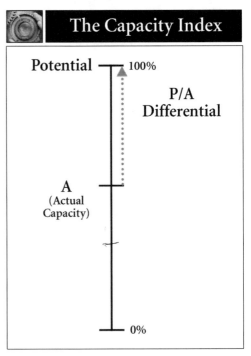

The Capacity Index

Potential — 100%

P/A
Differential

A
(Actual
Capacity)

0%

stands for *actual*. I realize that this process is highly subjective, so take a few moments to think before you mark your actual developed capacity. (No pressure, but remember that you are now expending finite psychic energy!)

The distance between the two marks is what I call your *P/A Differential*—the difference between what is possible for you and where you actually are. Most people place their A mark between 50 and 70 percent. But regardless of your P/A Differential, the important question is this: *what are you currently doing to increase the value of A?*

You cannot increase the value of A—your actual capacity—by wasting bits of mental energy. But you can choose to grow by purposely investing your psychic energy in activities that contribute to your physical, mental, social, and spiritual development. You can leverage this mental power into an expanded capacity and an increased quality of life. You can engage in a process of personal growth that will be repeated again and again throughout your lifetime, resulting in an upward spiral of continued development.

COUNTING THE COST OF DIMINISHED CAPACITY

What is at stake if you choose not to invest time and energy to increase A, your actual capacity? By now you've probably realized two things: the bits of mental energy that slip through the cracks in your mind are irretrievably lost, and they don't come from an inexhaustible supply. So if you choose not to use your mental energy purposefully, you're wasting a limited resource. But there's a greater loss. If you don't grow toward your full potential, *you will miss the chance to live out your dreams.*

Fourteen-year-old Homer Hickam faced this risk on a clear October night in 1957 when the Soviet satellite Sputnik traveled over his home in Coalwood, West Virginia. That night a dream was ignited in Homer's heart. The son of a coal miner, Homer dreamed of building rockets; he wanted to become an aerospace engineer. You may remember his story as told in the movie *October Sky.*

Young Homer's first rocket-building attempt was a dismal failure. Instead of streaming into space, the homemade craft blew up the garden fence. Homer's father, trapped by the limited expectations of small-town

West Virginia, dismissed the boy's dream as foolishness. But Homer refused to give up. He knew that if he would ever live his dream, he would have to grow. The A on his Capacity Index would have to move much closer to P if this coal miner's son would ever be transformed into an aerospace engineer. Homer recognized the need to educate himself about rocket science. Although he struggled with schoolwork, the power of the dream motivated him to learn.

Along with some friends, Homer eventually built a rocket that won first prize in a state science fair and a second rocket that won a gold medal in the National Science Fair. The national prize opened the door for Homer to study at Virginia Tech. He later worked for seventeen years as an aerospace engineer at NASA, where he helped to train astronauts and design Spacelab.

It is not particularly remarkable that fourteen-year-old Homer Hickam had a dream. It is remarkable that in spite of the tremendous odds against him, he invested his psychic capital wisely to create a rising orbit of personal growth. It is remarkable that he *lived* his dream.

You have a dream too, whether you have consciously recognized it or not. The question is, will you live your dream? The answer to that question hinges on your commitment to grow. Yes, the stakes are high—as high as Homer's October sky.

THE D/A DIFFERENTIAL

Let's return to the Capacity Index. You've already measured your P/A Differential, the difference between your maximum potential and your actual capacity. Now let's measure a third element, the capacity of your dream.

First, imagine your own October sky, a life-shaping experience that sparks a dream inside you. What is that dream? What do you aspire to be or to do? Next, place a mark on the Capacity Index that indicates your aspiration and label it "D" for *dream*. I believe your dream will always intersect with your Capacity Index at some point higher than A—your actual capacity. Dreams inspire us to reach beyond where we are. They command our attention, focus our thinking, and energize our actions. Dreams pull us upward into a higher orbit.

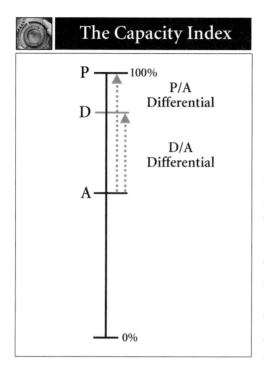

The distance between D and A on your Capacity Index is what I call the *D/A Differential.* And please understand the significance of this next sentence. *Your D/A differential is more important than your P/A differential.* If you don't fully grasp that sentence yet, go back and reread the previous paragraph. Now, the really, really big question is this: What will you do to close the D/A gap? That is the reality check of personal growth.

It is this unique relationship between dreaming and growing that sparked the title of this book, *The Dream Cycle.* I'll explain the Dream Cycle more fully in the next chapter, but for now, please understand why growing toward your potential is so important: your dreams are at stake.

WHEN DESTINY CALLS YOUR BLUFF

It seems that every movie Western has two obligatory scenes: a poker game and a gunfight. In the poker game, tension usually builds as we discover that one of the players is bluffing while the stakes continue to rise. The gunfight predictably follows when one player calls the other's bluff, bringing the game to a sudden end.

To say that you have a dream yet fail to grow is like bluffing in the poker game of life. It is pretending to be doing something that you really are not. The problem is that destiny never folds; it always calls your bluff. The time will come when you have to play your cards, make your move, seize the day. In that moment, if you have not demonstrated ownership of your dream by acting on a commitment to grow, you will be left with an empty hand.

Those who insist on pretending rather than growing transform their dreams into fantasies. They squander a hoped-for future in a world of make-believe.

Usually, that happens not because they risk everything, but because they risk nothing. To pursue your dreams will involve risk, perhaps even danger. But if you do not risk something by making the effort to grow, you will one day stare destiny in the face empty-handed. You will be left to wonder what might have been, if only you had been willing to act.

I remind you again: the reason you must keep growing is that your dreams are at stake. Thankfully, unlike old Hollywood Westerns, life allows an alternate ending. You write that ending as you choose to respond to the reality of your D/A Differential.

You don't have to sit there pretending. You can make your dream come true.

OUT OF THE COMFORT ZONE

A number of years ago, I had an amazing conversation with my eighty-five-year-old grandfather. I had called to see how he was doing one winter day, and the conversation went something like this.

"Well, it's been a busy day," my grandfather said. "I spent part of it shoveling snow off the roof."

"You what?" I couldn't believe my ears. Why would an eighty-five-year-old man be shoveling snow off a roof? I thought I detected a smile as he told me the answer.

"Somebody has to do it, you know. You can't just leave all that snow up there."

"But Gramps," I shot back, "what if you had fallen? You could have been hurt. Couldn't you get someone else to climb up on the roof?"

His chuckle both acknowledged that I was right and expressed a child-like glee at having accomplished the feat without difficulty. "Oh, I didn't want to bother anybody with something like that."

"Come on, Gramps," I was adamant now. "What were you thinking?"

His insightful answer placed so much of life into perspective. He said, "Seems to me I had a simple choice. I could either sit back and wait for the roof to fall in, or I could get up there and do something about it." I hung up the phone hoping I could climb even halfway up a ladder if I lived to be his age.

It is always easier to sit in a comfortable chair inside a warm house than to climb atop the house to shovel snow from the roof. It is easier to stay in any comfort zone than to venture out and try new and challenging things. But a comfort zone can easily become a rut—or even a grave. My grandfather knew that allowing a foot of wet snow to stand on an aging roof was a recipe for disaster. Of the two dangers, the risk of falling off the roof was the one he needed to take. I have to admit, I like the way he approaches life.

To settle for your present level of A—your current actual capacity—will always be more comfortable than to climb the ladder of personal growth to reach your dreams. But if you just sit there, taking a pass on the adventure of personal development, the weight of your dreams will eventually come crashing down around you. Yes, you will have to take some risks in order to climb the ladder toward your dreams. But consider the alternative.

So as you face the reality of your own D/A Differential, consider this: which risk are you going to choose, the risk that comes with doing something, or the far greater hazard of doing nothing?

LEVERAGE POINTS

1. If you have not already done so, create a Capacity Index and mark the value of A, your actual capacity. Reflect on your P/A Differential, the difference between your actual capacity and your maximum potential.

2. Think about your biggest life dream. Place a mark on your Capacity Index showing where your dream (D) intersects the Capacity Index. Consider the following questions based on the value of D and A on your Capacity Index:

   - If D=A, what does this say about the size of your dream?

   - If D>A, what does this say about your need to grow?

   - If D>P, how can you reality-test your goal to find out if it is a dream or a fantasy?

3. What system or process have you used over the last few years to address your D/A Differential? How effective has it been?

TWO

The Dream Cycle

Listening for the Future

I t has been said that the best way to teach a man to sail is to create within him a longing for the open sea. Why? Because dreaming of uncharted waters will motivate him to learn how to sail. Dreams have the power to shape our lives—especially if they are noble, selfless and God-inspired.

This book is focused on your personal growth. But since growing is always an uphill journey, you will need more than a part-time cheerleader or occasional pat on the back if you are to continue growing over a lifetime. Lasting personal development must be fueled by a reservoir of inner motivation, an underground river of desire that pumps life and energy to your journey. I believe you will find that source of power in your dreams.

Of all the possible sources of motivation, none is more powerful than a dream. In the wide-open spaces of your dreams, there are deep wells of motivation that you must tap into and drink from regularly if you are to endure the searing heat of the desert seasons through which your life will certainly pass. During those trying times, your dreams will sustain you.

THE NATURE OF DREAMS

The phrase "I have a dream" will be forever connected with Dr. Martin Luther King Jr., but the capacity to dream is universal. You can have a dream too; in fact, nearly everyone does. What is a dream? Simply this: *a compelling awareness of what could or should be, accompanied by a growing sense of responsibility to do something about it.*

It is important to note that both a *compelling awareness* and a *sense of responsibility* must be present in order for unfocused (or perhaps even subconscious) passions to emerge as dreams. Reflect on the words of Dr. King, spoken so passionately on August 28, 1963.

> I have a dream that one day this nation will rise up and live out the true meaning of its creed: "We hold these truths to be self-evident: that all men are created equal." I have a dream that one day on the red hills of Georgia the sons of former slaves and the sons of former slave owners will be able to sit down together at a table of brotherhood. I have a dream that one day even the state of Mississippi, a desert state, sweltering with the heat of injustice and oppression, will be transformed into an oasis of freedom and justice. I have a dream that my four children will one day live in a nation where they will not be judged by the color of their skin but by the content of their character. I have a dream today.

King's life had a power that transcended the eloquence and passion of his words because he married the essence of his dream—a compelling awareness of what should be—to a sense of inner responsibility for making it so. When your heart truly connects with a God-inspired dream, you tap a pipeline of inner motivation that will both inspire your personal development and enable you to endure hardship. There is a vital, symbiotic relationship between dreaming and growing. There is no richer source of fuel for the engine of self-directed growth than your dreams.

THE DREAM CYCLE

The paradox of dreams is that they are both powerful and fragile. Untold thousands of potentially world-changing ideas float through the minds of people every day. But very few of these thoughts ever amount to anything. Some are forgotten nearly as fast as they are imagined. Others survive long enough to be discussed, but talking is not the same as dreaming. Other ideas become dreams but never mature because they are not accompanied by a sense of responsibility. The vast chasm between idea and reality is the graveyard of unrealized dreams. Perhaps those dreams will rise again in the heart of another dreamer, but unless they are energized by a willingness to act and undergirded by a plan for achievement, they will be destined to die once again.

If you will grow to become the person you long to be, you must accept the responsibility for making your dream a reality. To help in understanding this progression from dreaming to doing, I've developed a schematic called the *Dream Cycle*. There are two initial phases to the dream cycle. Phase 1 comprises the steps of *Listening, Processing,* and *Dreaming*. These activities are *fueled by* receptivity, inquiry, and possibility. Phase 2 involves *Planning, Doing,* and *Realizing*. These activities *result in* a strategy, activity, and reality. Let's look at each component in more detail.

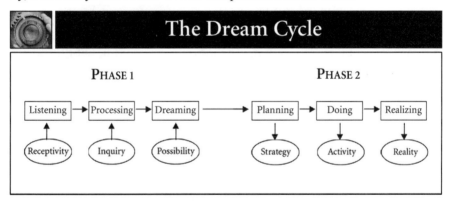

Listening

Dreaming begins with listening. You discover your noblest dreams when you listen to your soul's deepest longing or hear the resounding echo of a God-inspired cause in the cathedral of your heart. That's why *receptivity* is critical for this stage of the Dream Cycle: receptivity feeds the Listening process. When you are receptive to God, you connect with the sovereign purpose He had in mind when he created you. Then, like a message in a bottle, dreams begin to wash up on the beaches of your soul.

In the history of ancient Israel, there is a powerful object lesson on the importance of listening. The story begins with these cryptic words: "In those days the word of the LORD was rare; there were not many visions."[1] We know that the God of Israel often communicated through dreams and visions. But at this time in history, the leaders of Israel were not receptive to God's voice—they weren't listening. One small boy, however, was able to hear the voice of God.

Samuel was a boy who lived at the house of the Lord, assisting Eli, Israel's high priest. One night after Samuel had gone to bed, he heard a voice calling for him. Samuel quickly rose and presented himself to Eli. But Eli said, "I did not call; go back and lie down."[2] Three times Samuel heard the voice and ran to Eli; each time Eli told him to go back and lie down. Finally, the old priest realized that God might be trying to speak to the boy, so he instructed him to respond to the voice, should he hear it again, with the words, "Speak, LORD, for your servant is listening."[3]

God did speak again, and Samuel responded as instructed. What he heard was a powerful message telling of momentous changes that would soon take place in the land. *What is* was about to be replaced by *what should be*—and only Samuel knew it because only Samuel was listening.

But what makes this story so ironic is that the message God gave to Samuel was not intended for him. The message was for Eli, but Eli had not been listening. Because of his failure to listen, Eli became a marginalized leader, sitting on the sidelines at a critical moment in his nation's history, void of any opportunity to influence others.

If you want your life to be about something more than yourself, if you want to add value to the lives of those around you and leave behind something worth remembering, start listening. Listen to the passions that bubble up from the well of your heart. Listen to the hurts, hopes, and longings of the people around you. Listen to the causes and concerns that rise up from the pages of history in which you are living. A receptive, listening heart is the fertile ground in which dreams take root.

Processing

Dream seedlings are often surrounded by a swirl of questions. Where did this come from? Why me? What am I supposed to do? How can I make a difference? Who is going to help me? When should I start?

The list goes on, and each question is likely to spawn several more. You cannot ignore them. You must consider them, investigate them, and, ultimately, answer them. This is the Processing component of the Dream Cycle, the time when you engage in a self-discovery that tests the viability of your dream. *Inquiry* is the critical aspect of this component because it fuels the Processing function. Failure to engage in this process will leave your dream standing like a tree without roots. When tested by a storm, it will come crashing to the ground. The likelihood of your dream's survival is proportional to your level of confidence as you emerge from a diligent process of inquiry.

This is not, however, a purely cognitive experience. Processing includes an emotive, soulish journey through the valley of decision. Like a complex computer network, the mind, will, and emotions exchange mystical data while the monitor screen of the heart displays an hourglass icon saying, "This may take a while." Usually, it does. But when the churning subsides, you will emerge from the Processing phase with a newly installed dream and a burning desire to make it happen.

Dreaming

Dreaming, ultimately, must move beyond vague ideas to a concrete goal. Dreams must be more than an unfocused visceral urgency to do "something." They must be sufficiently defined so that they form the basis of a plan. A dream is a clear picture of the future. The formation of that vision takes place in the Dreaming component of the cycle. This is where the dreamer visualizes what could be in place of what is. The key word for this component is *possibility* because possibilities fuel the activity of Dreaming.

When Dr. King said "I have a dream," he was able to articulate the essence of the dream—what should be—in personal, down-to-earth terms that touched the hearts of common people. His ideas were not locked in ivory towers or confined to the hallways of academia. Dr. King's use of the statement "I have a dream" was always connected with practical examples. As a result, his dream reverberated across the country like the boots of an army, pounding rhythmically toward victory. The dark reality of what is was swallowed up by the bright light of what should be. When you emerge from the Dreaming component, you will have a clear picture of *what should be* in your future.

Planning

Planning begins Phase 2 of the Dream Cycle, the stage where dreams are translated into reality. Dreams must mature into a plan if they are to come true. A dream is like a train, and a plan is the track. No engine, no matter how powerful, can move a train without a track. Every dream must have a plan.

That is why every dreamer needs a planner. Sometimes the dreamer and the planner are the same person. Sometimes they are dream partners, sharing a common passion. The result of effective planning is a *strategy* that maps out how the dream will come true.

Planning flows in part from the Processing component of Phase 1. Processing refines the values that will serve as boundaries for the plan, just as banks limit and direct the flow of a river. Dr. King, a man of deep personal faith, was influenced by the life of Mahatma Gandhi. Gandhi's emphasis on nonviolence shaped the planning of the civil rights movement and anchored it to the moral high ground. King's dream became something more than an idea as it was connected to an agenda, a plan that could harness the previously untapped potential of the many people who believed in the cause.

Doing

The logical expression of planning is doing. The Doing component of the Dream Cycle produces *activity*. Thomas Edison said, "The value of a good idea is in using it." Plans are essential in the Dream Cycle. But the best plan in the world is useless until someone finds the courage to act upon it. More than one dream has been aborted *after* a good plan was in place because no one had the commitment or confidence to follow through on it.

In 1905, when Albert Einstein first published *Relativity: The Special and General Theory*, he provided ideas that formed the basis of a plan to build nuclear reactors and, eventually, a nuclear bomb. At the time, few people were aware of Einstein's publications, but the whole world changed forty years later when his ideas were developed and acted upon. The power of a plan is released by action.

Action almost always calls for sacrifice. Sacrifice tests the depth of one's commitment to a dream. It exposes fraudulent dreamers who want a medal without a battle, a stage instead of a foxhole, recognition without resolve. True dreamers understand that the currency of suffering and opposition may be the necessary deposit for a later return.

Realizing

Combining the right ideas with the right actions over the right period of time will enable you to realize your dream. The Realizing component of the Dream Cycle results from the cumulative effect of Doing over time. Your dream becomes *reality* when you consistently act upon your strategy.

That reality, however, may be slightly different than what you expected. Many people—and perhaps you—will view the reality of your dream in terms of what you have achieved. Those closest to you, however, will view that reality in terms of your character. The value of your realized dream will always be measured by an index of your achievements and your character. Although I am separated by time from Martin Luther King Jr., I know that he had a dream, and I know what that dream was. King's dream was, at least in part, realized. He created a new reality. Yet a man of lesser character could not have spoken the words of Dr. King or leveraged the same results. Likewise, your accomplishments will be framed by your dreams, but they will be built upon the foundation of your character. The strength of your *being* will dictate the impact of your *doing*.

The reality that you create through your Dream Cycle will be built largely from your *life dream*. That life dream may not be a single dream, but may comprise several dreams from different stages of your life into one, overarching dream. A *life-stage dream* is an age-appropriate cause or goal that has both stand-alone value and developmental benefits. Few young leaders will be remembered for the life-stage dreams they pursue along the way, but these worthy causes help shape their character and expand their capacity for what is to come. Your life dream, however, is much larger and flows from the essence of your being and purpose—who you are and why God placed you on the earth at this moment in history.

On the surface, the sequence of Listening, Processing, Dreaming, Planning, Doing, and Realizing seems to be a complete cycle. It moves from idea to activity to accomplishment; from beginning to end. But something very important is missing. There is another phase—a *hidden phase*—of the Dream Cycle, one that shows why it is so urgent that you keep growing. We'll uncover that hidden phase in chapter 3.

LEVERAGE POINTS

1. Review the definition of a dream on page 24. Based on this definition, what are your most prominent dreams? If you have not already done so, write a simple description of the tension between *what is* and *what should be* as defined by your most prominent dream. (For additional help with formulating your dream, review the Dream sub-section of the Personal Growth Assessment tool available free at www.KeepGrowingInc.com.)

2. Does your description go beyond identifying the problem that needs to be solved and envision the possibility of what should be? If not, what possibilities do you envision?

3. Are these the dreams you were thinking of when you completed the Capacity Index at the close of chapter 1? If not, where do these dreams intersect with your Capacity Index?

4. Review the Dream Cycle diagram on page 25. Where do you feel you are now with regard to the dreams you listed above? Which component of the Dream Cycle do you need the most help with?

5. Think of dreamers you know personally or have studied from history. Do you observe that their dreams unfolded in the pattern of the Dream Cycle? What can you learn from their journey?

THREE

Beneath the Surface

Hidden Challenges to Your Dream

Although never seen by most people, the ground beneath the city of Chicago is alive with activity. A network of streets that never see the light of day plays host to an endless stream of trucks that resupply the city's stores. Plumbing, gas, and electrical lines course along the hidden foundations of the sparkling towers that form the familiar skyline. Remove this hidden underground, and the city would shut down.

Something similar is true of the Dream Cycle. The components that appear on the surface—Listening, Processing, Dreaming, Planning, Doing, and Realizing—must be supported by a network of four hidden components. Without these often overlooked elements, the Dream Cycle will not culminate in the desired results.

THE HIDDEN PHASE

What are these unseen components, and why are they so important? They are Growing, Sharing, Timing, and Finishing, and they are vital because *they overcome the challenges that would prevent you from realizing your dreams.* Let's examine each component of the Hidden Phase of the Dream Cycle. As we do, we'll see that each one addresses a challenge you must face if you are to move from where you are now to the desirable future of your dream.

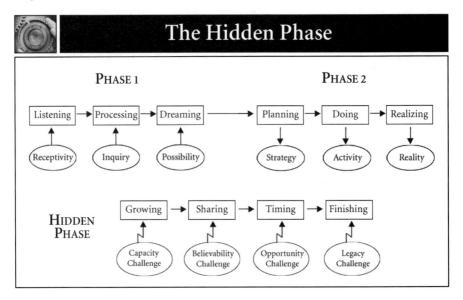

Growing

The bigger your dream is, the wider will be the gap between your present capacity and the capacity you will need in order to act upon it. On the Capacity Index, we measured this gap as the difference between D (your dream) and A (your present actual capacity). The D/A Differential represents your first challenge in realizing your dream, your *capacity challenge*.

If there is no gap between your present capacity and the capacity you need in order to realize your dream, one of two things must be true. Either your dream is not very big, or you are in the latter stages of your life, riding the wave of many years of personal growth. Remember, dreams always intersect the Capacity Index at a point higher than A, your actual capacity.

The only way to conquer the capacity challenge is to keep growing. If you don't grow, you will never have the ability to live your dreams, regardless of how noble they are or how well you have planned. There are some aspects of the Doing stage of your dream that you can complete now. But there will most likely be important items on your dream's to-do list that you simply do not have the capacity to accomplish—and never will if you don't grow.

This tension between D and A, Dream and Actual, is the result of what Richard Boyatzis describes as the first two discoveries of self-directed learning. The first discovery is my ideal self, what I want to be. The second discovery is my real self, who I am. These two discoveries expose both my strengths and my needs—what I've described as the capacity challenge. In order to realize my dream, a bridge must be built that spans the distance between the ideal and the real. That bridge is *personal growth*. The design of the bridge is a self-directed *growth plan*, a learning agenda, which Boyatzis calls the third discovery of self-directed learning.[1] Creating this agenda for learning is like building a pipeline that pumps life-giving motivation from the reservoir of your dream into your current situation.

Growing is the first critical component of the Hidden Phase of the Dream Cycle. If you do not grow, you will never have the capacity to achieve your goals and realize your dreams. You must have a personal growth plan to overcome your capacity challenge.

Sharing

There is a second challenge that you must overcome in order to realize your dream: the *believability challenge*. In order for your dream to be doable, it must be believable. Certainly, you have to believe in your dream. You can never perform consistently at a level beyond what you believe is possible. No one can. You must have a plausible vision of the future in order to move toward it. You must believe in your own dream.

Yet you are not the only one who must buy into your dream. No dream worth pursuing can be realized by you alone. Therefore, you will have to share your dream with others and enlist their help. They, too, must believe in your dream. This is the Sharing component of the Dream Cycle.

Believability is closely linked to capacity. If others cannot see that you have the capacity to achieve your dream, they will not respond when you share it with them. Since you know that your present actual capacity is insufficient to accomplish your dream, you may feel trapped in a catch-22. You do not have the capacity to achieve the dream, but if others do not see that capacity in you, they won't help you move forward.

So how do you solve the dilemma?

You keep growing, and you do it openly. You grow in a way that others can see evidence of change in you and will credit you with the *future capacity* that is now only potential. The believability of your dream is equal to your actual capacity plus your *rate of growth*.

Capacity is the key that opens the door of believability and invites others into your dream. That's another reason you need to keep growing. If you do not increase your capacity, no one will believe in your dream.

Timing

The third component of the Hidden Phase is Timing, which focuses on *opportunity*. This is a crucial component of the Dream Cycle, and it is critically linked with two other stages, Sharing and Doing. If you share your ideas too soon, before you have developed the capacity to overcome the believability challenge, people will not buy into your dream. They may even actively oppose you or otherwise discourage you from moving forward. You must have the right opportunity to share your dream. Timing is critical.

Timing also plays a role in the Doing portion of the Dream Cycle, since you will need to discern which parts of your plan to tackle now and which to save for another day. The excitement and passion you have for your dream may actually work against you here. It takes great discipline and restraint to keep from doing too soon. It is important to have the right window of opportunity for each action. A great plan can be foiled by implementing it at the wrong time.

Often, there is a gap between our *desire* to act and our *readiness* to act. This is what I call the *opportunity challenge*. Two biblical characters provide vivid examples of this challenge and underscore the importance of timing in realizing our dreams. The first is a young man named Joseph.[2]

As a boy, Joseph had a God-inspired dream that he would become a leader. He was given a vision that portrayed him at some future time as having such stature that his entire family would bow to him in respect. Though Joseph did not fully understand the meaning of this dream, he naïvely shared it with his brothers and father. They saw Joseph as a braggart and took offense at the notion of his future authority. Many years later, Joseph rose to second-in-command of all Egypt, and his family did bow before him. But sharing his dream at the wrong time only fueled the rivalry between Joseph and his brothers. They sold him as a slave to a traveling caravan, a betrayal that began a long and painful journey for Joseph in Egypt. It took a lifetime for Joseph to realize the importance of timing.

Moses is another biblical character who illustrates the Timing component of the Dream Cycle.[3] Many years after Joseph died, Moses, an Israelite, was born in Egypt. The Israelites were now under the thumb of their Egyptian masters and were suffering greatly. Moses was supernaturally spared from death as an infant and raised by Pharaoh's daughter. He grew up among the ruling class of Egypt. Yet Moses began to empathize with his own enslaved people. One day he saw an Egyptian taskmaster beating a Hebrew slave. In a moment of rage, Moses killed the Egyptian and hid his body in the sand. Moses thought his own people would welcome him as a deliverer, but they did not. His murderous act surfaced, and Moses was forced to hide from Pharaoh in the desert. Moses was correct in wanting to deliver the Israelites from slavery, but his Doing was stained with the blood of untimely zeal. It would be forty years before Moses got another chance to act upon this dream.

Clearly, Timing is a crucial element in realizing any dream. But how do you know when to take action? Five principles will help you decide. First, when the time is right, you will *become obsessed with the dream.* The experience of a dreamer is not unlike that of an expectant mother. During pregnancy, a mother may move from initial excitement to discomfort to a period of normalcy. Finally, discomfort builds again, culminating in labor pains that become more intense and frequent until the child is born. In acting upon your dream, don't mistake the initial excitement that follows the conception of the dream for the labor pains that immediately precede its culmination. If you are "pregnant" with a dream, the time will come when it is impossible to hold it in any longer.

Second, you will know the time is right when you have *a sense of preparedness.* Mild anxiety about what lies ahead will be overridden by a sense of destiny that whispers, "You were made for this." Like Israel's King David, you will face the giants before you with a realization that the same divine source of strength that enabled you to "kill a lion and a bear" will enable you to prevail.

Third, you will know the time is right because you are guided by credible *mentors who believe in you.* Wise counsel is invaluable in discerning the right time to act. Be careful not to mistake casual comments such as "sounds like a good idea to me" for credible evaluation. If none of your mentors are prepared to say "I believe in you" based on a thoughtful analysis of your plan, you may be moving too soon.

Fourth, proper timing will be indicated by *peers who support you*. Big dreams require big teams. You will need the support of people who are prepared to roll up their sleeves and go to work. Attaining a critical mass of human capital is a good sign that your time has come.

Finally, you will know it is time to act when you have *people who will follow you*. If your dream is worthwhile, it will add value to the lives of others. When your desire to act resonates with their desire for change, a window of opportunity will open.

Timing is a vital element of the Dream Cycle. Without proper timing, your dream will not succeed. By seizing the right opportunities, you will realize your dream. How will you recognize the proper timing? You must keep growing.

Finishing

Finishing is the final hidden component of the Dream Cycle, and it concerns your *legacy*. The legacy that you leave behind will be based on the fulfillment of your dream—what I have called Realizing. But your completed dream and your legacy will not be identical. Your legacy is more than what you have and what you have done. It is also who you are and how you finish.

Leaving a rich legacy depends upon finishing well, and the odds are against you. Research on leaders from biblical and church history has documented the fact that few leave a positive legacy. In fact, according to Dr. Robert Clinton, only about one in three leaders finish well.[4] The odds in the marketplace may be even worse. From Enron's corporate fraud, to the Catholic Church's sex-abuse scandals, to the headlines of the local paper, we are bombarded with real-life reminders that it is difficult to achieve great things, maintain integrity, and finish well. Many capable people who have had worthy dreams have failed to leave a positive legacy because they could not overcome flaws in their character. This is the *legacy challenge*—the difference between achievement and character, the gap between doing and being.

The usual barriers to finishing well are not surprising: pride, power, money, sex, family problems, and a failure to keep growing. Yet many leaders do overcome these pitfalls. Dr. Clinton's analysis of leaders who have left a legacy reveals five activities that enhance one's ability to finish well.

The first is repeated renewal experiences that deepen one's faith and keep life centered on a relationship with God. Clinton found those who repeatedly sought such were far more likely to leave a positive legacy.

Second, leaders who finished well had a solid network of relationships that significantly influenced their lives. They had accountability partners and close friends who provided a relational safety net in times of testing.

Third, positive leaders developed the virtue of self-discipline. This disciplined lifestyle enabled them to remain true to their core beliefs, especially in the areas most important to them.

Fourth, they had a long-term perspective that enabled them to view the twists and turns of their life's journey against the backdrop of the big picture.

Fifth, they were lifelong learners. They did not come to a personal growth plateau and remain there; they kept climbing.

All five of these finishing enhancements are important for anyone who hopes to leave a legacy of realized dreams. Of the five, perhaps the last one—lifelong learning—is most crucial because it encompasses several of the others. As you continue to grow, you will expand and strengthen your network of significant relationships, begin to take a long-term perspective on your life, and shore up your personal discipline. In pursuing your dreams, it is never enough to run well or even to achieve great things. You must finish well. And in order to do that, you must address the inner issue of character—you must continue to grow.

STAGES OF LIFELONG GROWTH

We've discovered four significant challenges to realizing any dream. Each one corresponds to one component of the Hidden Phase of the Dream Cycle.

- *The Capacity Challenge*   The gap between your present capacity and the capacity you must develop

- *The Believability Challenge*   The gap between what others see in you and your potential

- *The Opportunity Challenge*   The gap between your desire to act and your readiness to act

- *The Legacy Challenge*   The gap between what you do and who you are

Each of these challenges can be overcome in only one way—by *intentional, lifelong learning.* You need to keep growing because you don't presently have the ability you need to realize your dreams. You need to keep growing because others will not support your dream unless they see that you are growing to develop the capacity to reach your full potential. You need to keep growing in order to develop the wisdom to discern the proper time to act. Finally, you must develop character, supportive relationships, and self-discipline so that you will finish well and leave a positive legacy for those who follow you.

Overcoming each of these challenges is required for realizing dreams, and each challenge should be a powerful motivation to grow over a lifetime. The urgency for growth in each area, however, will likely change over time. Younger leaders tend to have a high concern for believability but give little thought to capacity, less to opportunity, and none to legacy. Armed with the zeal that flows from a dream, they are loaded with self-confidence—and they need it. But youthful self-confidence may lock reality in a back room and stifle the voices that warn of challenges in capacity and opportunity. Most young dreamers are primarily concerned about being taken seriously. They want someone to believe in them now.

Motivation for Growth over a Lifetime

Age 20	Age 40	Age 60
Believability	Capacity	Legacy
Capacity	Opportunity	Capacity
Opportunity	Believability	Opportunity
Legacy	Legacy	Believability

Over time, the connection between capacity and believability becomes clear. If other people are going to believe in you enough to join you in this dream-laced journey, you need to demonstrate that you are capable of leading the way. The more you develop the necessary plans to pursue your dream, the clearer the picture you will have of what needs to be done. That picture serves as a reality check, reinforcing the connection between capacity and believ-ability. It also introduces the issue of timing. Opportunity becomes more important, as you realize the need to choose carefully when to act. The middle game of the Dream Cycle stimulates a higher felt need for capacity and opportunity. It also provides a glimpse of the future, which adds legacy to the mix.

In the final season of the Dream Cycle, your focus shifts quite naturally to legacy. As dreams are being realized, you will tend to think more about your long-term contribution and how you will be remembered. You will have received enough payoff from the habit of purposeful growth that you will not abandon it. But capacity and believability issues will diminish in intensity. Legacy becomes the dominant concern.

Where you need to grow right now will depend on where you are in the Dream Cycle. That you need to keep growing is certain. The focus of that growth will shift as you move through life and make progress toward your dreams.

THE DREAM CYCLE IN ACTION

Let's review the Dream Cycle, both it's surface and hidden phases. First is Phase 1, in which the dream takes shape in your heart. Phase 1 begins with Listening. In this stage, you hear from God, tap into the passions He has placed in your soul, and see how they connect with the needs around you. You will emerge from this phase with a growing sense that things could or should be different than they are. The next stage is Processing. Dreams don't come with instruction manuals. Once embraced by a listening heart, a dream must be shaped and fueled by the creative inquiry of the dreamer. Processing will refine your dream, giving you a sense of where you will go, where you will not go, and what you will need in order to get there. Then comes the time for full-blown Dreaming—envisioning possibilities and forming a mental picture of *what could be* as a beneficial replacement for what is. At the close of this stage, you will have formed your vision for the future, your dream.

Phase 2 begins the transition from thought to action. That begins with Planning, the stage in which you develop a strategy for achieving your dream. You must have a plan in order to carry your dream into the future. Next comes Doing, the time when you take action based on your plan. The right actions based on the right plan over the right period of time will result in Realizing. That is the stage at which your dream becomes a reality and your legacy takes shape.

Remember that the visible phases of the Dream Cycle must be supported by the four components of the Hidden Phase: Growing, Sharing, Timing, and Finishing. In order to bridge the gap between your dream and reality, you will have to keep growing, enlist the help of others, seize the right opportunities, and stay the course to finish well. Without these crucial elements, your dream cannot succeed.

That's a snapshot of the Dream Cycle, but what does it look like in real life? History provides many examples of dreamers who mastered the three phases. Probably none exemplifies the power of dreaming better than a young man who was born in a small village near Paris, France, nearly two hundred years ago. Louis Braille is a picture of the Dream Cycle in action.

Blinded by an infection as a child, Louis often wandered in fields near his home or sat by the pond, playing games of his own invention. Father Palluy, the village priest, observed Louis's curiosity and invited him to his home for lessons several times a week. Father Palluy read Bible stories to Louis and told him about the wonders of nature that were no longer visible to him.

Louis did so well with his lessons that Father Palluy asked the local schoolmaster to allow the boy to attend classes with the sighted children. Louis excelled in everything that involved memorization. If he could listen to the lecture and memorize the information, he had no trouble understanding. But much of the schoolwork included reading and writing, which left Louis sitting idle. Yet while his hands were still, Louis's mind was active. As he listened to the scratching of the other students' chalk on their writing slates, he began to make a connection between what is and what might be. He began to dream about the possibility of reading and writing.

Sometime later, Louis moved to the Royal Institute for Blind Youth in Paris. There he heard of a system of *nightwriting* developed by Captain Barbier of the French army. Nightwriting was a combination of dots and dashes punched into a piece of cardboard, which enabled frontline soldiers to communicate in complete darkness without making a sound. Barbier had come to believe his system could enable the blind to read and write.

Louis began to process his dream by experimenting with Barbier's system. But the young man soon discovered that the system had a serious flaw. Since it was based only on sounds, there was no consistent method of spelling, punctuating, or forming numbers. And because the French language includes so many sounds, the system was very complex. Most of Louis's fellow students became discouraged and gave up on the idea completely. Louis, however, decided to modify Barbier's system by simpifying it. He shared his ideas with Dr. Pignier of the Royal Institute, who passed word of Louis's efforts along to Barbier. The captain asked for a meeting to explore Braille's ideas in person.

When Louis met with Barbier to discuss modifications to the system, he faced the believability challenge head-on. As a young blind boy, he didn't have the credibility to convince Barbier of the problems that kept his ideas from being effective. While admitting that the process perhaps needed slight modification, Charles Barbier refused to budge on the basic premise that the dots and dashes should represent sounds.

Motivated by the power of his dream, Louis refused to give up. Instead, he renewed his commitment to keep growing, and he began planning a system that would make raised-dot communication practical. Over the next few months, Louis made good progress, but he couldn't settle on a system that was simple enough to be "read" with one quick touch of the finger. Then Louis asked himself this question: what would happen if the dots and dashes were used to represent letters? That single breakthrough insight was a paradigm shift Barbier had been unwilling to make.

The idea of moving from sounds to letters expanded Louis's capacity, enabling him to develop a functional system. By the fall of 1824, he had been working on his ideas for three years. He was now able to record dictation and then read it back. That expanded capacity was enough to overcome the believability challenge—at least for the moment. Louis requested a meeting with the director of the Royal Institute. He sat opposite Dr. Pignier's desk with a writing board, paper, and stylus in his hand. He asked the director to select any passage from a book on his shelf and read it slowly, just as he would while dictating to a sighted person. Dr. Pignier began to read, and Louis encouraged him to go faster as he carefully punched dots with his stylus.

Upon completing the passage, Louis turned the paper over, ran his fingers across the raised "letters," and read the passage back word for word. Dr. Pignier was amazed. He immediately took another book and repeated the experiment. Once again, Louis perfectly recorded the passage and read it back. In no time, the entire school was treated to a similar demonstration. Louis Braille was only fifteen years old.

The Braille system swept through the Institute, finding enthusiastic acceptance among the students. Louis was asked to remain after graduation to serve as a teacher. He excelled, and so did the students. Their opportunities for learning had grown exponentially now that they could read and write.

Unfortunately, the outside world was still stuck in the past. The only reading method for the blind approved by the French government was an outdated embossing system based on tracing oversized letters to form words. Dr. Pignier tried to get government officials to adopt the Braille alphabet, but the wheels of bureaucratic change turned very slowly. Eventually, Louis had the opportunity to give a public demonstration of his system for the king of France and the minister of the interior, who had the authority to approve the Braille alphabet. They observed politely, asked a few questions, and left. Louis never heard from them again.

In 1840, Dr. Pignier was replaced as director of the Royal Institute. The new director, Armand Dufau, wanted to avoid taking risks. He feared that the move to Braille from the old embossing standard would separate blind people from the sighted world because Braille used a totally different alphabet. He banned its use and confiscated the students' slates and styluses.

Dufau had authority to ban the official use of Braille at the Institute, but he could not remove it from the hearts of the students. They used nails, pencils, pins—anything they could find—to punch dots on paper. They kept diaries in Braille and taught new students how to use it in secret. Louis was torn. He could not openly rebel against the director, but he knew the students would never turn back. Was it the right time to act?

The silent war between the students and the director finally ended when Joseph Guadet became assistant director. He quickly discovered the tension in the Institute and met with Louis as well as individual students. Guadet readily saw the advantages of the Braille system. Braille's plan for written communication was clearly superior to embossing, and Louis had demonstrated the capacity to mainstream his method. Guadet now shared that dream. He lobbied the director, convincing him that the Braille alphabet could not be held back forever. Would he really want to be remembered as the man who tried to stop a great invention developed by a student in his own school?

Armand Dufau was motivated to grow, change, and risk—something he had been unwilling to do before—because of concern for his legacy. On February 22, 1844, a large crowd gathered for the dedication of a new facility. Many changes were in the works, including the admittance of girls to the Institute and a name change to the National Institute of Blind Youth. Dufau chose this grand occasion to promote the formal adoption of the Braille system by the Institute.

Guadet read a pamphlet to the large crowd explaining how Braille worked. Then he staged a dramatic demonstration in which a volunteer from the audience read a poem while a blind girl copied down the words. A second blind girl, who had been kept out of earshot, then read the poem with her fingers, reciting it aloud to the audience. A government official in the crowd objected, saying that the second girl could easily have memorized the poem in advance. Gaudet invited the official to read anything he chose in a repeat of the demonstration. The government official fished around in his pocket, found a used theater ticket, and read aloud the name of the play, the theater, and details of the show. As he read, a blind girl recorded the information using Braille. The second girl returned, moved her fingers over the raised dots, and read exactly what had been dictated. The crowd broke into spontaneous applause!

Louis Braille had realized his dream. Now, every time you enter an elevator or hospital room you will see the system of raised dots that was created by a teenage boy who had a dream to communicate. His legacy lives on.

Regardless of where you are in the Dream Cycle, like Louis Braille, you must keep growing if your dreams are to come true. You have powerful reasons to keep growing, but there are formidable barriers that stand in the way of your personal growth. In the next chapter, we will turn our attention to the most common barriers you will face as well as the practical steps to overcoming them.

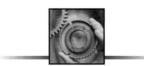

LEVERAGE POINTS

1. Review the Hidden Phase diagram on page 32. Which aspect of the Hidden Phase—Growing, Sharing, Timing, or Finishing—is most important for you right now? To what degree have you previously underestimated the interdependency of these four components?

2. What are the most important areas in which you need to expand your capacity if you are to realize your God-inspired dreams? How might you turn your capacity challenge into a source of inner motivation to grow?

3. How does the D/A Differential relate to the Timing component of the Dream Cycle? How much of your own D/A Differential can you realistically erase in one year?

4. Review the five principles for determining correct timing on pages 35–36. Apply them to your dominant life dream. What does this tell you about the Timing component of your dream?

5. Review the Motivation for Growth diagram on page 38. In which phase of growth do you see yourself? Which of the four challenges—capacity, believability, timing, and legacy—provide the most motivation to grow? What changes, if any, should you make to your personal motivational hierarchy?

FOUR

Change Dynamics

Breaking the Status Quo

In order to realize your dreams, you must grow. And growth demands change. Therefore the Dream Cycle will never be complete in your life until you experience personal change. I cannot stress this point too much: *you must change in order to realize your dreams.*

Change is synonymous not only with growth but also with life. In the words of author Leonard Sweet, "A clinical definition of death is a body that does not change. Change is life. Stagnation is death. If you don't change, you die. It's that simple. It's that scary."[1]

Change is that simple because it is part of life. Your own body is an example of this. Your skin replaces itself every month; the stomach lining, every five days; the liver, every six weeks; the skeleton, every three months; cheek cells, three times a day. Ninety-eight percent of the atoms in your body are replaced every year—your whole body is replenished every five years (for men) or seven years (for women). Change is life. It's that simple.

Change is scary, but the alternative is death. We live in a rapidly changing world. Postmodern culture has an incredibly high rate of change, and leaders must be prepared to deal with it constantly if they are to remain relevant and effective. One of the implications of this rapid change rate is the need for habitual, proactive learning. If you are not committed to a cycle of continuous growth, you will soon find yourself losing touch, dying a slow death. Change is life; stagnation is death. It's that scary.

The good news is change is possible. You have the capacity to change because you have the ability to grow. This is something you can do. The bad news is that change is not easy. There are powerful forces that work against your personal growth, and you must be prepared to confront them if you are to expand your capacity and realize your dreams. While our bodies are in a constant cycle of change, our emotions tend to fight against change in an effort to protect the status quo—even when that is less than desirable. Think about how many times you have said out loud that you really ought to get in better physical condition or that you ought to learn a new software program or develop a hobby that has been on the back shelf of your mind for years.

Why haven't you followed through?

Your answer might include a number of complex factors, but the heart of the reason is that you—like everyone else—have an innate preference for the status quo. You would rather maintain your comfort zone than expend the effort it will take to change. It's true that most of us would prefer the *results* of change to the status quo, but we prefer the status quo over the *effort* required to bring about change. In order to realize your dreams, you must overpower the inertia of the status quo and overcome the barriers to personal growth. You must change.

THE DYNAMICS OF PERSONAL CHANGE

Many people have attempted to understand and explain the dynamics of personal change. One of the clearest models of change theory was developed by the German-born psychologist Kurt Lewin.[2] Lewin stated that in order to change, we must first unfreeze the status quo by recognizing the undesirability of the present situation and the benefits of transformation. Ironically, Lewin further realized that if a change is to last, it must culminate in a refreezing that integrates new beliefs or behaviors into a newly formed status quo. The status quo, Lewin added, is maintained by equilibrium between two opposing forces: *driving forces* and *restraining forces*. As long as the restraining forces are equal to or greater than the driving forces, no change occurs.

Based on Lewin's thinking, a sensible approach to personal change is to begin by evaluating the *force field* that affects your situation—the driving forces (which favor change) and the restraining forces (which resist it). Once those forces are clearly in focus, it is easier to clarify the actions that are required to complete the three-step process of unfreezing, changing, and refreezing.

The most efficient way to initiate change—the second of Lewin's three steps—is to simultaneously increase the driving forces and decrease the restraining forces. For each of your personal growth goals, there will be both driving forces and restraining forces. In fact, right now there is something holding the present level of A (your actual capacity) in place on your Capacity Index. If there weren't, you would be experiencing spontaneous growth all the time—just like the cells of your body. So in order to unfreeze the status quo, you must identify and increase the driving forces while you identify and decrease the restraining forces.

Since your growth goals are unique, it is impossible for this book to address all of the driving and restraining forces that may be at work in your situation. Yet there are several big-picture forces that operate in nearly every person's life. Once you understand these common driving and restraining forces, you'll be able to conduct your own *force field analysis* and specifically address the forces that affect you. First, let's examine the common restraining forces.

COMMON RESTRAINING FORCES

My experience as a trainer and personal growth coach has enabled me to identify several restraining forces that affect nearly everyone. I have grouped these forces into three general categories. They are forces that affect *consistency, complacency,* and *competency.* In order to unfreeze the status quo, you must learn to decrease each of these forces. Let's identify the specific forces in each of these categories and then take a look at how to counteract them.

Consistency Forces—Identifying Them

I have coached many people who appeared as though they really wanted to grow. Their desire was so intense that they took the time to produce a personal growth plan, but their follow-through was so intermittent that progress was difficult to measure. The forces driving their desire to grow were not strong enough to overcome the restraining forces of inconsistent action. Two factors seem to be at the heart of inconsistency: lack of personal discipline and poor time management.

Personal Discipline. I believe that personal discipline is a function of the will and therefore can be disassociated from personality or temperament. I have met people from every corner of the personality chart who have passed the acid test of personal discipline—making and keeping promises to themselves. Self-discipline and organizational ability, however, are not the same thing. Right-brained, creative types can grow on purpose in spite of the fact that they may struggle with personal organization. The approach they take looks quite different from that of left-brain, analytical thinkers, but the result is the same—personal transformation.

Since personal growth requires self-directed learning, there is no replacement for personal discipline. Growth over time is more about grunt work than glory. Harry Truman said, "In reading the lives of great men, I found that the first victory they won was over themselves . . . self-discipline with all of them came first."

Time Management. The second restraining force in the consistency category is poor time management, which is a first cousin of poor self-discipline. Discipline relates primarily to the will; time management is a skill. They are built one upon the other, like a house on its foundation. Time management skill yields only marginal results without an appropriate measure of personal discipline behind it.

One of the most common excuses I hear from people who want to grow but are not doing so is that they are too busy. Often, these are people who have a personal growth plan. They simply don't follow through on it because they don't seem to have the time. Yet we know from the Dream Cycle that planning unaccompanied by doing bears no fruit. Someone has said that hope is not a strategy. I would add that good intentions are not a replacement for disciplined action. You cannot daydream your way out of the status quo.

Consistency Forces—Counteracting Them

Since time management is a skill, it can be learned, and there is a wealth of tools available. But what if you already have a FranklinCovey planner, the latest PDA, and a thousand Post-it note messages littering your workspace, but you still can't seem to use your time efficiently? Perhaps the foundation of effective time management—personal discipline—is the missing link. If so, you probably don't need a highly paid consultant to diagnose your problem. You simply must determine to do something about it.

Realign your values. The first step in attacking a discipline problem is to recognize it as a symptom and not a cause. The root problem of discipline—and much of what is passed off as poor time management—is actually a misaligned value system. To get to the heart of your discipline problem, you must admit that the problem is with your values and priorities, not your willpower or schedule. Does that cause you to do a double take? I'll say it again: your values and priorities are the real problem.

Let me explain that statement. If you lack the discipline to manage your time and follow through on growth goals, you are making the tacit admission that something else matters more to you than personal growth. It's that simple. The ultimate commentary on your values is your behavior. Imagine a conversation with a friend who tells you he really wants to get out of debt. He feels pressure from every direction, and the situation seems desperate. You respond by referring him to a financial counselor. A week later, you see your friend and ask how things went in the debt-management consultation.

"Not so well," he says.

"What happened?"

"You wouldn't believe what she told me," your friend continues incredulously. "She actually wants me to cut up my credit cards, get a less expensive car, and live on a budget. I want to get out of debt as much as anybody, but that's crazy!"

So, what is the real problem here? Ultimately, it comes down to values.

The same is true with your time management problem. Until you rearrange the hierarchy of your values and give priority to personal growth, it is unlikely that you will ever reduce consistency-related restraining forces enough to produce long-term change. And unfortunately, changing your values is often more difficult than changing your behavior.

So now what?

In order to raise the value of something in your life and give it a higher priority, you need to move beyond the question of *how* to the questions of *what* and *why*. When you focus on why something is important and what the long-term results will be, it is easier to press through the details of how you will act upon it.

In a personal growth coaching session with a leader (I'll call him Bob), I came to believe that he was face-to-face with a restraining force that blocked his desire to get into better physical condition. He had developed a well-defined growth goal, but inconsistency ruined his progress. I challenged Bob with the notion that his discipline problem was really a value problem. I wanted him to think more about the *what* and *why* associated with his goal. His family had a history of heart problems, and he had recently been to the doctor for a checkup. The doctor confirmed that unless Bob dropped thirty-five pounds and adjusted his diet, his chance of dying from a heart-related illness was very high. I knew that Bob's wife was pregnant with their first child. So my conversation with him began something like this:

"Bob, as important as the details of your plan are, you need to get beyond *how* you are going to grow and start thinking about *why*. You need to focus on the long-term ramifications of growing or not growing in this area."

Bob nodded. I continued.

"Think about your unborn son for a minute." I paused. "Do you want to be there when he graduates from high school and college? Do you want to share in the joy of his wedding day and play with your grandchildren? Do you want to grow old with your wife and share a fruitful life of serving others?"

"Of course I do," Bob responded quickly. "I want all of those things."

Having identified the *why* of Bob's plan, I leveraged it's power in rearranging his values. "Bob, that's what you need to focus on in order to rearrange the pecking order of your values. If you're going to stir up the discipline to push away from the table and get regular exercise, you need to think about your son."

Do you think that conversation was blunt? I do. But as a result, Bob took steps to increase his accountability for this goal and renewed his commitment to counteract the forces that were restraining his growth. Sometimes the only way to get over the hump is to deal with the hard, cold facts.

Aron Ralston found himself staring at a cold reality on May 1, 2003. The discipline that he summoned is truly amazing, and it powerfully illustrates what a person can endure when he looks beyond the question of *how* to *what* and *why*.

You may not be able to place Aron's name, but you will probably recall hearing his story. On Saturday, April 26, 2003, he set out for a routine day of climbing in Utah's Canyonlands National Park. The twenty-seven-year-old Aspen resident had proven himself an avid outdoorsman and expert climber, having conquered forty-nine of Colorado's 14,000-foot peaks. This climb was to be a warm-up for Alaska's Mount McKinley.

Ralston parked his truck near the base of Blue John Canyon and took off on a fifteen-mile bike ride. After tying his mountain bike to a tree, he began his technical descent into the canyon. He planned to drive the truck back to get his bike. While maneuvering through a tight spot in the rock face, Ralston placed his hand next to a large boulder. Without warning, the boulder shifted onto his hand, trapping him there. He did everything he could to move the boulder, but it weighed several hundred pounds. It wouldn't budge.

On Tuesday, three days later, Aron ran out of water. He was also running out of options. By Thursday he had spent four nights in the open with temperatures dipping into the thirties. At midday, Aron accepted the fact that he could not separate the boulder from his hand; he would have to separate the hand from his arm. The only tool he had was a pocketknife. First, Aron broke the bones in his forearm so that his knife could cut through the flesh. Then he applied a tourniquet and completed the grisly task of amputating his own hand. The "operation" took about an hour.

Incredibly, after cutting off his own hand, Ralston rappelled more than sixty feet down the canyon! Then he hiked some four miles before finding a vacationing family, who called for help. When Sgt. Mitch Vetere helped Aron into the rescue helicopter, he was within a mile of his truck. According to Vetere, most people would have given up; Ralston refused. Although the *how* of escape seemed impossible, he focused on the *what*—his certain death if he didn't escape—and the *why*—the fact that he desperately wanted to live to climb another day. Although Aron Ralston valued his hand, the priority of staying alive took precedence over keeping it.

The trade-offs you will have to make to follow through on your dreams are not likely to be this dramatic. Even so, you will probably need to re-order your values in order to defeat the restraining forces that would keep you rooted in the status quo.

Generate Momentum. A second step to acquiring personal discipline is to harness the power of momentum. John Maxwell has described momentum as the great exaggerator. You look better than you are when you have it and worse than you are when you don't. Momentum speeds you toward your dream. In order to generate momentum, you must choose your growth goals wisely, recognizing that you cannot do everything at once.

The difference between a mediocre organization and a great organization is rarely one or two major practices. More often, the difference is created by "a thousand little things" that any organization could do if it really wanted to. The same is true of individuals. The difference between you and another more fruitful leader of similar capacity is rarely one or two major issues; it is more likely a host of simple steps you could take if you so chose. None of those "thousand little things" is overwhelming when taken alone, but viewed cumulatively, they can be paralyzing. So in order to create momentum, you must concentrate on a few of them at a time. With even a modest string of personal growth successes under your belt, the resulting combination of newfound discipline and time management skill will help you create new habits that accelerate your growth.

Consistency forces don't have to hold you back forever, but you must confront them. If you don't, they will grow into a set of more serious problems—complacency forces.

Complacency Forces—Identifying Them

Complacency is a state of self-satisfaction accompanied by an unawareness of dangers or deficiencies. Complacency, as it relates to personal growth, is actually a survival reflex that kicks in when we attempt to unfreeze the status quo.

Complacency is not our natural state, however. Most people do not want to remain trapped in less-than-ideal circumstances. Healthy children do not need to be coaxed to dream about what could be, and they have a natural bent toward learning new things. One writer made this assessment: "From [ages] four to five we are all romantics; we are all embryonic royalty, budding ballerinas, or intrepid astronauts; we are all fearless, open, affectionate, and beautiful."[3]

Yet over time, the restraining forces of complacency increase in strength, choking out the natural inclination to change and grow. In spite of an underlying thirst for growth, we eventually come to accept where we are. In an attempt to block out the dangers and deficiencies of the status quo, we drink an intoxicating cocktail of complacency and denial. What are the restraining forces that make us complacent? I could cite many, but I will offer the two most prominent ones that I have observed while coaching leaders.

Past Failures. First, past failures in the area of personal growth tend to wear us down until, like fatigued climbers, we accept the view from our current plateau as "good enough." We quietly relinquish our hold on the ultimate goal of reaching our highest potential.

As I have talked with people about the importance of personal growth, many of them have admitted that past attempts were unsuccessful. That negative track record becomes a powerful restraining force, making the status quo appear to be the lesser of two evils—staying where they are and making another doomed attempt to grow.

Emotional Wounding. A second restraining force associated with complacency is emotional wounding. Childhood curiosity and the willingness to try new things wane in direct proportion to our awareness of what other people think about us as we venture in new directions. Most of us have at least one childhood memory of being jeered by other kids as we tried something new but failed to deliver the expected results. There is a Charlie Brown hiding inside of almost everyone, reeling over the public laughter of a Lucy-like figure, reluctant to step forward again.

If you have endured a childhood of demeaning comments that heightened your insecurities, making you feel that you will never amount to anything, you have a powerful restraining force to overcome. Those childhood sound bytes have become such a part of your mental landscape that they may affect your willingness to change even now, long after you have forgotten who spoke them. Under these circumstances, even the slightest attempt at personal growth is like paddling a canoe against the raging force of a swollen mountain stream.

Complacency Forces—Counteracting Them

To fight against this powerful current, you must decrease the restraining forces of failure and emotional wounding. You can't change the past, but you can change the way you think, which, in turn, impacts how you feel. That makes it easier for you to change your behavior and grow on purpose. Emotional wounding from past failures may seem overwhelming, but it can be overcome. At the risk of oversimplifying what can be a very complex journey, consider these three steps to reducing the restraining forces of complacency.

Accept Unfairness. First, accept the fact that life is not fair. Good people sometimes get sick and die young. Someone with fewer qualifications and less experience may be hired instead of you. A tree may fall to the left and damage your car instead of falling to the right and landing in an open yard. If you accept the fact that "stuff happens," you can free yourself from many of the negative emotions that spin out of control when you suffer injustice.

Accept Failure. Second, realize that failure is part of the journey. When I hear people use the "I've tried before and failed" excuse for not growing, I want to look them in the face and say, "So what? Of course you have tried and failed. Who hasn't? What does your past failure have to do with anything in the future?"

In order to reduce the restraining force of failure, you must begin to view failure differently. Many personal growth attempts that have been labeled failures could just as easily be described as minor progress. It's a matter of perspective. When you learn to grow on purpose (as I'll describe in Part 2 of this book), you will greatly reduce the number of fits and starts in your growth journey. But failure will never be completely removed from the equation. It would be foolish to stop growing because you have failed before or will fail in the future.

Recapture the Power of Choice. Third, to overcome the forces of complacency, you must intentionally recapture the power to choose. There are many aspects of life over which you have little control. But one thing no one can take from you is the power to choose how you respond to the unexpected twists and turns that come your way. No matter how deep are the hurts inflicted by others or the bitter failures you have brought on yourself, you still have the power to choose. Take control of your attitude, and begin to record new mental sound bytes to replace the negative messages that fuel your complacency.

Perhaps the simplest and most powerful way to replace self-defeating thoughts is to plant seeds of affirmation in other people. One of the byproducts of encouraging those around you is the rewiring of your own mind. This is the Law of the Harvest, which is described in the Bible. Simply put, you reap what you sow.[4] If you sow positive thoughts into others, you will reap a positive attitude in your own mind. So take the focus off yourself, and begin to encourage others. Look for ways to affirm them, speak positively about them, and become an ally in their growth. Being others-focused will help you break free from the restraining forces that have kept you chained to the status quo.

Probably no person exemplifies the power of choice better than Sir Douglas Bader of the British Royal Air Force. In 1931 he lost both of his legs in a flying accident. It would have been easy for Sir Douglas to resign himself to a life of self-pity, thinking of what might have been. Instead, he took charge of his thoughts and focused his energy on learning to use his artificial legs. Not satisfied with just walking, he wanted to fly again. During the Battle of Britain, Sir Douglas Bader became a flying ace with twenty-two confirmed kills.

In 1941 Bader was captured by the Germans after his plane collided with an enemy aircraft. The crash destroyed one of his artificial legs. Sir Douglas's German captors so deeply respected his courage that they asked the Royal Air Force to airdrop a new pair of legs for him. After receiving his new legs, Sir Douglas attempted escape—four times! After the fourth attempt, the Germans decided that he couldn't be trusted to stay put and began to confiscate his legs each night and return them each morning.

Take a page out of Sir Douglas Bader's life story by choosing to rise above your failures, challenges, and complacency-laden status quo.

Competency Forces—Identifying Them

My use of the term *competency forces* includes two situations that are nearly opposites. In some cases, lack of competency is the problem; in others, ironically, competency *is* the problem. Both sides of the competency coin can incite restraining forces that perpetuate the status quo.

Lack of Competency. Lack of competency—and perhaps inexperience—in developing a personal growth plan makes it more difficult to pursue self-directed learning. Rarely will the lack of skill in developing a personal growth plan, as a single restraining force, prevent you from changing. But if that lack is combined with the restraining forces of complacency and consistency, it can have a piling-on effect. The good news is that if you are motivated, you will find a way to grow in spite of an imperfect growth plan.

Higher Competency. While it may be difficult to think of competency as a restraining force, it is true that it brings its own set of problems and can blur one's perspective as easily as failure. Some people are highly competent in other areas of life (besides personal growth), and their success generates enough fulfillment to diminish the felt need for improvement. High competency in any area of life brings affirmation and satisfaction. That can be dangerous when a leader allows satisfaction with present results to replace a healthy dissatisfaction with the status quo. A plateaued leader is flirting with danger. Celebrating current victories is a healthy practice. Reflecting on past victories is also an important means of marking progress and recognizing those who have helped along the way. But when celebration and reflection are allowed to squelch the passion for continued development, they become restraining forces that stand in the way of change.

Competency Forces—Counteracting Them

Much of the rest of this book describes how to build competency and experience personal growth. In Part 2, you will learn how to create and implement a personal growth plan, so if lack of competency is a restraining force in your life, read on. For now, however, here are a few suggestions for diminishing the restraining forces associated with competency.

Keep Your Eyes on the Future. First, make it a habit to celebrate present victories against the backdrop of future goals. You have probably heard post-game interviews with professional athletes who tempered their celebration of a playoff victory with the recognition that it was not the ultimate win—they continued to look forward to the championship game. Even after a team wins the highest prize in a given sport, it soon regroups around the challenge of repeating the feat, recognizing that such an achievement will require an even higher level of growth.

While you celebrate present victories, verbalize your statement of where you are against the backdrop of where you are going, and recommit yourself to continued growth. Don't allow the celebration to drag on and blur your vision of what is yet to be accomplished.

Associate with Higher Achievers. Second, go out of your way to associate with people who are a level beyond you in capacity development and personal accomplishment. Let their life example serve as a reminder that you have not yet arrived, and let it be a source of motivation to keep growing.

One of the more creative ways to associate with high achievers is to study the lives of great men and women who have gone before, leaving a model life as an example for us to follow. I recently studied the life of G. Campbell Morgan, a great British preacher of the early twentieth century. His disciplined study habits and knowledge of the Bible challenged me to press on in my own faith journey. Comparing myself with this great man, I found myself thinking that after years of study, I know hardly anything about the Bible! His life example inspires me to persevere in my own study habits. This process of historical mentoring is so important that I have dedicated the entire next chapter to three profiles of personal growth.

The most common restraining forces that work against your desire to change will probably come in the areas of consistency, complacency, and competency. As you decrease them, you will begin to unfreeze the status quo so that you can change.

But there is more. You must simultaneously increase the driving forces that favor change in your life. Let's find out what they are and how to maximize them.

COMMON DRIVING FORCES

For most people, the driving forces for change come from the Dream Cycle itself. If you have noble, God-inspired dreams stirring in your heart, you will have the strongest possible desire to change the status quo and make a positive impact on the world around you. There are other sources of motivation, such as personal survival or selfish gain, but over a lifetime, your dreams provide the most important driving forces. Like ocean waves beating relentlessly against the shore, your dreams push against the status quo, driving you to change in order to reach them.

Identifying Driving Forces

The specific driving forces in your life will always be linked to the four challenges of the Hidden Phase of the Dream Cycle: capacity, believability, opportunity, and legacy. Although these challenges represent liabilities, your awareness of them becomes a driving force in each area. As you realize where you need to grow in each area, you will be driven to change so that you can pursue your dream. The intensity of each driving force will differ based on a variety of factors including your place on a developmental timeline, but it will be your desire to expand in these four areas that drives your personal growth.

As a leader moving into the "middle game" of life, my strongest driving force relates to capacity, so I leverage my strengths to bear on the most crucial aspects of my life mission. And since I am very legacy conscious, I also concentrate on character issues and the behaviors that enhance my ability to finish well. Those are the forces driving change in me right now. The driving forces may be slightly different for you, but regardless of your season in life, you must tap into your dreams as the source of power to unfreeze the status quo. What is your dream for the future? The answer to that question will drive the changes in your life.

Increasing Driving Forces

When you analyze your Force Field in connection with the Capacity Index, you will begin to see the connection between the size of your dream and the power of your driving forces. To increase your driving forces, you must increase the power of your dreams.

The restraining forces in your life are pushing against your present level of A (actual capacity). In order to unfreeze the status quo, you will have to identify and reduce them. At the same time, you must increase the driving forces that flow from D (your dream).

There is a direct relationship between the strength of the driving forces that flow from the Dream Cycle and the D/A Differential on your Capacity Index. A higher D/A Differential presents a greater challenge in the areas of capacity and believability; it also suggests the presence of a large life-dream, which is more likely to be tied to your legacy. Therefore, the larger the D/A Differential, the more powerful will be the driving forces that flow from D and the more likely it will be that they can unfreeze the status of A. That will result in an increased capacity and continued personal growth. But, the most important point to be made here is that if you want to increase your driving forces, keep dreaming—and dream even bigger dreams!

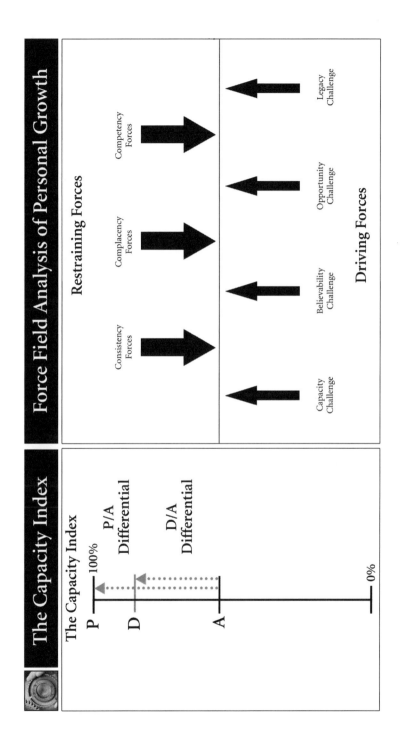

GROWTH PARTNERS AND THE GOD FACTOR

There are two additional allies available to you in your struggle to create personal change. One is the friendship you have with people who can become your personal growth partners. A network of supportive relationships is one of the most powerful means to simultaneously reduce the restraining forces and increase the driving forces in your life. I'll say much more about that in chapter 10, which is dedicated to the role of growth and accountability partners in your personal growth plan.

Remember, too, that no one wants you to grow more than God does, who created you. As you seek to overcome the forces that fight against your personal development, draw on the strength that only God can provide through prayer. Ask Him to help you become more disciplined, to heal the wounds of your past, and to renew your mind. Open yourself to the dreams God has for you, and ask Him to give you the faith to pursue them. Ultimately, personal growth isn't about you; it is about God working in you and through you to accomplish His purposes. In the words of Saint Paul, "There has never been the slightest doubt in my mind that the God who started this great work in you would keep at it and bring it to a flourishing finish on the very day Christ Jesus appears."[5]

So, don't forget the God factor!

LEVERAGE POINTS

1. If personal growth is individualized change management, how might your attitude toward change or your change history affect your efforts in personal growth planning?

2. Review your history of personal change, both successes and failures. In each case, what does the outcome of your efforts reveal about the *what* question—what you value most?

3. Review the diagram on page 59, then do your own Force Field
    Analysis, showing the specific restraining forces that are holding back
    A, your actual capacity. Use the size of the arrows to demonstrate the
    strength of each driving and restraining force.

4. What specific steps could you take to simultaneously increase your
    driving forces and decrease your restraining forces?

FIVE

The Dream Team

Learning from Historical Mentors

W illiam Carey had a dream. On October 2, 1792, the thirty-one-year-old
pastor attended a meeting with some fellow ministers in
Northampton, outside of London, hoping to share his vision. For six
years Carey had been urging the formation of an organization to send
missionaries overseas. He had written an eighty-seven-page booklet
outlining the biblical and factual basis for his plan. In previous meetings,
he had communicated his passion by preaching from the words of the
prophet Isaiah, "Enlarge the place of thy tent . . . thy seed shall inhabit
the Gentiles. . . ."[1] Carey summarized his message in this phrase, which
has been repeated by dreamers ever since: "Expect great things *from*
God. Attempt great things *for* God."

Up to this point, however, Carey's associates did not share his dream of
forming a society focused on sending missionaries to foreign lands. During
this October 2 meeting, Carey sensed the same doubt and uncertainty in the
air, and he feared that the gathering would end with another postponement.
So he decided to use a different approach, hoping it would communicate his
passion and help others share his dream. Carey challenged his fellow
ministers with the story of a great leader who had gone before them, Count
Zinzendorf of the Moravian Brethren.

As a young leader in his early twenties, Zinzendorf had made his property in Moravia available as a refuge for those suffering persecution under England's Counter Reformation and the oppressive acts of King Charles VI. Although they were a small group, the Moravians experienced a powerful revival and eventually began sending missionaries all over the world.

Carey had read accounts of the Moravians' endeavors in periodicals printed in 1791. He used their example of dedication and commitment to inspire his fellow Baptists to take action. And, by the grace of God, it worked. The first Baptist missionary society was formed out of that October meeting.

Carey's dream was realized. But his legacy had only begun.

Fourteen years later, in August of 1806, a group of students from Williams College in Massachusetts gathered along the banks of the Hoosack River to pray. Samuel Mills was among them. On their way back to campus, the students were caught in a rainstorm and sought shelter under a haystack. Their conversation turned to the needs of the world and what they, as students, might do about them. The same sense of doubt and uncertainty that had plagued Carey's colleagues filled the air at this impromptu meeting. But Samuel Mills, who had read Carey's eighty-seven-page booklet, challenged his peers to action. Their motto became "We can do this if we will." William Carey's dream was reborn in their hearts.

With Mills and other young leaders as its driving force, an American missions society was formed six years later. On February 19, 1812, the first American missionaries set sail for India, where they would join hands with William Carey.

Part of the legacy of great leaders is the inspiration they provide, sometimes unwittingly, for those who follow them. Zinzendorf and his Moravian Brethren served as a historical model for William Carey. William Carey's life and writings became a source of motivation for Samuel Mills. C. T. Studd, another missionary hero, spoke of his final charge into the heart of Africa with these inspiring words: "Gentleman, God has called me to go, and I will go. I will blaze the trail, though my grave may only become a stepping stone that younger men may follow."[2] There is tremendous power in the example of a great leader.

In this chapter, you will meet three dreamers whose lives are models of personal growth: D. L. Moody, J. Hudson Taylor, and John R. Mott. By sharing their stories, I hope to inspire you to a lifetime of dreaming and doing. And—perhaps more important—I hope to motivate you to find historical role models of your own. These men are three of my heroes. If you are to realize your dreams, you will need a growing company of your own historical mentors who will become a cheering "crowd of witnesses" that push you forward in your journey.

D. L. MOODY

Dwight Lyman Moody was born on February 5, 1837. His father died when Moody was four years old. Moody's earliest correspondence shows that he either was inattentive in school or suffered from terrible teachers; he had only three or four years of formal schooling.

As a young man, Dwight Moody got a job at a shoe store in Boston. On April 21, 1855, Moody's Sunday school teacher, Ed Kimball, came to the store on a clear mission to convert Moody to Christ. He delivered this simple message to the young man: "I want to tell you how much Christ loves you." Moody put his faith in Christ that day, at the age of eighteen.

Moody later moved to Chicago and started a Sunday school, sharing God's love with poor and underprivileged children. His methods were unconventional, which earned him the nickname "Crazy Moody." Although he was never ordained or seminary trained, at age twenty-three, Moody abandoned secular employment to enter full-time Christian ministry. He became a city missionary for the YMCA, and he served in a chaplain-like role with the U. S. Christian Commission during the Civil War—all of this before beginning his career as an evangelist.

Sometime later Moody visited Ireland. In a park in Dublin, a fellow evangelist remarked that "the world has yet to see what God can do with a man fully consecrated to Him."[3] This single sentence captivated Moody and gave birth to the dream that would guide his life, to become that man. From that point on, Moody had a remarkable career as a Christian evangelist. He preached to more than one hundred million people—*before* the advent of radio or television—and founded a church, a Bible institute, and a publishing house. How could a man with so little formal training accomplish so much? In addition to his amazing natural abilities and the "God factor," D. L. Moody had this advantage: he was a lifelong learner.

Ask Questions

Moody never let his lack of education become a stumbling block. Instead, he turned it into a bridge, using that disadvantage as the motivation to learn from anyone God put in his path. In 1861, at age twenty-four, Moody was asked to give a lecture on urban Sunday schools to pastors and church leaders in Peoria, Illinois. One minister recalled that soon after Moody was introduced to the other ministers, he turned to one of them and asked, "How do you explain this verse in the Bible?" quoting the verse word for word.[4] Most of his interaction with the group consisted of Moody quoting Scripture and asking these better-trained theologians for sound interpretation.

Seek Mentors

Moody engaged mentors whenever possible and made the most of the people God brought into his life. While in England, he sought out the famous preachers George Mueller and Charles Spurgeon. He invited top leaders and communicators such as G. Campbell Morgan, F. B. Meyer, A. J. Gordon, Hudson Taylor, and Andrew Murray to speak at the conferences he hosted for students in Northfield, Massachusetts. Moody actively participated in these meetings and took extensive notes as the great men spoke.

Reflect on Experiences

Moody took time to reflect upon his experiences and learned much from the school of life. His ministry experiences during the Civil War proved that Christians could work together and that professional clergy were not the only people who could do God's work. Having been marginalized by many of the clergy in Chicago, Moody later refused ordination. He believed that his reputation spoke for itself. He thought also that by being known simply as Mr. Moody (rather than Reverend Moody), he could encourage other lay people to become active in Christian work.

Listen to Others

As a speaker, Moody worked to stay in touch with the needs of his audience. He organized a special meeting called the Question Drawer during each of his evangelistic campaigns. Attendees of the Question Drawer would write a question on a piece of paper and place it in a box that was passed around the room. Moody, always working with several local pastors, would draw out a question, but he always deferred to the local clergy for an answer before offering one of his own. This system allowed him to learn what was on the minds of the people attending his services, and he adjusted his preaching topics and illustrations to address their needs more directly. Moody also listened carefully to the answers the area pastors gave, viewing this as an opportunity to further his own theological education.

Study Consistently

Moody was hungry for knowledge all of his life. He said, "One man may have 'zeal without knowledge' while another may have knowledge without zeal. If I could have only the one, I believe I should choose the first."[5] Moody believed that the primary source of knowledge is the Bible. R. A. Torrey recounted a time when he stayed with Moody at his Northfield residence. At 5:00 a.m., Moody tapped on Torrey's door to see if he was awake. Torrey said, "I happened to be; I do not always get up at that early hour but I happened to be up that particular morning. [Moody] said, 'I want you to go somewhere with me,' and I went down with him. Then I found that he had already been up an hour or two in his room studying the Word of God."[6] Moody knew that if he was to find time to study he would need to get up before other folks do. He had learned the value of a disciplined approach and applied it faithfully to his own life.

J. Hudson Taylor

Another peer from whom Moody learned much was J. Hudson Taylor. James Hudson Taylor was born on May 21, 1832, in Barnsley, England. His father was a Christian, a chemist by trade, and a local Methodist preacher. Hudson was converted to Christianity at age seventeen when he read a tract from his father's library. That same year, concerned about his tendency to lose religious fervor, Taylor cried out to God for the grace to remain faithful. He emerged from that encounter knowing that he was called to serve others in China.

The whole of Hudson Taylor's life played out against the backdrop of this divinely given life-dream. He served in China for fifty-one years, eventually founding a new mission society focused on the interior of the country. By the time of his death in 1905, China Inland Mission had established 20 mission stations, brought 849 missionaries to the field, and trained an additional 700 Chinese workers. Some estimate that Hudson Taylor baptized 50,000 Chinese people, as many as 35,000 of them being people he had personally converted to Christ.[7]

Hudson Taylor left a legacy unequalled in the field of modern Christian missions. Where did he find the capacity to realize such a powerful life-dream? He, too, was a lifelong learner.

Prepare Carefully

From the moment he initiated his Dream Cycle by listening to a divine call to serve in China, Hudson Taylor began to learn in preparation for acting on his dream. In 1850 very little was known in the West about China, but Hudson Taylor heard about a book written by Dr. Medhurst of the London Missionary Society. Told that a Congregational minister in his hometown had a copy of the book, Taylor managed to borrow it and found in it helpful information about the training he would need to serve effectively in China.

Learn from Failure

Taylor also learned from failure. He began his journey as a missionary with the Chinese Evangelization Society (CES), arriving in China a few months before his twenty-second birthday. By 1856 he resigned from the CES due to a litany of problems, not the least of which was their failure to provide him with a consistent salary. Based on advice from George Meuller, Taylor committed himself to a lifestyle of radical faith, trusting God to supply his financial needs. Taylor had also been frustrated by the bureaucratic structure of CES. All decisions had to be approved by the mission's leaders in England, and Taylor had seen many opportunities come and go because action could not be taken promptly.

In 1860 Hudson Taylor returned to England. By the summer of 1865, he was convinced that if he were to realize his dream of working in the interior of China, a new mission society would have to be formed. Processing gave way to dreaming and planning, and Taylor mapped out an operating strategy for a new organization, China Inland Mission (CIM). Notice how this strategy was shaped by Taylor's ability to learn from experience, including what we would call failure.[8]

Inclusion. First, Taylor believed that the CIM missionary force should not be limited to one denomination. Members would embrace a simple statement of Christian doctrine that would provide the platform for their unity. While other agencies were seeking to recruit ordained or university-trained missionaries, Hudson Taylor was convinced that God could use those with little education if their hearts were right. He was also open to recruiting women and giving them a greater scope of ministry than might have been expected at that time. These were bold and innovative steps, as was CIM's eventual inclusion of workers from countries outside of England.

Trust. Second, CIM would be a faith mission, providing no guaranteed salary. All of its members would share the group's income and look to God to supply their needs and operate without debt. This operating principle was a clear response to Taylor's problems with the financial dealings of CES. In addition, the newly formed CIM would not appeal directly for funds or publish the names of donors. Having been influenced by George Mueller, Hudson Taylor adopted a *faith mission* approach.

Delegation. Third, again in reaction to the administrative structure of CES, Taylor determined that CIM would be field directed; he would take initial leadership responsibility and then involve other leaders onsite in China. They simply would not permit the delays and inefficiencies of communication with England to slow the work in the field. Taylor also believed that many situations were too complex to be processed accurately by home-office officials.

Outreach. Fourth, the mission would share the love of God in all of China, beginning with beachheads in strategic centers. The day he committed himself to form this new mission society, Taylor prayed for twenty-four willing workers and noted this in the flyleaf of his Bible. This number was derived from the eleven provinces of China plus Tibet, which was an independent country at the time. These volunteers would give themselves to making converts, establishing churches, and training leaders without concern for whether the new disciples were formally connected with CIM. The goal was to help people experience God's love and forgiveness, not to advance the organization of CIM.

Acculturation. Fifth, CIM missionaries would dress like the Chinese and worship in buildings that reflected local architecture. Taylor had discovered during his earlier stint in China that western dress could be a serious barrier to building relationships with the Chinese. Ignoring the sneers of more-experienced missionaries, Taylor donned traditional Chinese dress and adopted a Chinese hairstyle. He led the mission in eliminating every possible hindrance to effective communication with the local people.

With the benefit of hindsight, we can readily see how effective Hudson Taylor's plan was. It is amazing that he was only thirty-three years old when he created this strategy and that his primary training had been a "failed service" in China. That "failed service" shaped Taylor's values, increased his capacity, and laid the foundation for one of the most effective missionary efforts the world has ever seen.

JOHN R. MOTT

On May 25, 1865, one month to the day before J. Hudson Taylor formed China Inland Mission, a future Nobel Peace Prize winner named John Raleigh Mott was born in Livingston Manor, New York. Like Taylor, John Mott's legacy is a testimony to the value of lifelong learning.

John Mott moved with his family to Iowa, where at age sixteen he enrolled in a small Methodist preparatory school. In 1885 he transferred to Cornell University with dreams of a career either in law or in his father's business. The following year a famous British cricket player by the name of J. E. K. Studd (the brother of C. T. Studd) came to Cornell to challenge students with a description of the "Cambridge Seven," who had rejected fame and riches to serve as volunteers with Hudson Taylor's China Inland Mission. John Mott was a late arriver at the first meeting, getting to his seat just in time to hear these words: "Seekest thou great things for thyself; seek them not. But seek first the kingdom of God."[9] The message confirmed what God had already been saying to him and served as the anchor point for his commitment to a life of Christian ministry.

In July of 1886, John Mott attended a summer conference organized by Dwight Moody in Northfield, Massachusetts. Listening to other students, Mott learned the importance of foreign missions and soon joined their efforts to mobilize one hundred of the attendees for overseas service. From this student gathering came the momentum of the Student Volunteer Movement, of which Mott would serve as chairman for thirty-two years. He also served the YMCA, whose original purpose was to share God's love through fitness and recreation programs.

Under Mott's leadership, nearly 20,000 students went overseas as missionaries. Although he never served as a long-term missionary himself, Mott circled the globe mobilizing others. He crossed the Atlantic more than one hundred times, and for fifty years he averaged thirty-four days per year on the ocean. He helped organize the World's Student Christian Federation in 1895 and presided over the 1910 World Missionary Conference in Edinburgh. His statesmanship and influence gained him global credibility and recognition, culminating in the 1946 Nobel Peace Prize.

Mott, like Moody and Taylor, was a purposeful learner. His appetite for learning was driven by his sense of destiny and life dreams. He often challenged students to recognize that it is important to "link up your life to a great cause." Having a God-inspired dream of his own, Mott always retained the inner drive to grow. What were his methods?

Establish Disciplines

As a young student, Mott adopted his own set of Benjamin Franklin–like rules for life that addressed physical, mental, social, and spiritual well-being. He regularly attended Methodist class meetings, which were small group meetings for spiritual growth and accountability. He retained this disciplined approach to personal growth all his life and emphasized to students the importance of daily, unhurried study in the "choicest time of the day." For Mott, that time was the start of the day, the "Morning Watch," a title he borrowed from a movement at Cambridge.

Read Constantly

As a widely sought communicator, Mott sensed the need to remain relevant and in touch with current thought. He was a lover of books, devouring the writings of the best scholars of his day in a variety of disciplines. He routinely wove ideas and illustrations from his reading into his speaking.

Mott's intense travel schedule provided him with extended blocks of time for reading and reflection. On long trips across the ocean, he was known to bring along "an entire library." While en route to Africa in 1906, the steamship company gave him an extra cabin just for his books, and he spent hours at a time poring over them. Some days he would read an entire book in the morning before moving on to correspondence. When seasick, Mott had his traveling assistant read to him.

Adopt Heroes

John Mott was greatly inspired by the lives of those who had gone before him. As a young man, he discovered the power of biography, reading about the great British revivalists John Wesley and George Whitefield. In 1890 Mott visited the birthplace of American missions, Williams College, where Samuel Mills had studied. In 1894 Mott stood in the home of the great reformer John Knox, where "those great Reformation thunderbolts" had first been kindled.[10] Some time later Mott lingered in the very room where Martin Luther had translated the New Testament and Psalms. These heroes of the faith were a source of motivation and encouragement, pushing him to expand his own capacity to dream and achieve.

Establish Accountability Partners

John R. Mott also benefited from associations with contemporaries like Luther Wishard and Robert Wilder, who provided him with encouragement and accountability. Mott organized an annual Quiet Day, a meeting with a few peers that was augmented by a monthly circular, much like a personal newsletter. When together, Mott and his associates would share books they had read, plans for the future, and heart-level concerns. This inner circle of relationships became a lifelong fellowship.

Associate with Giants

Mott's many travels exposed him to the world's best thinkers and Christian leaders, but no mentor more powerfully impacted his life than did D. L. Moody. This is what Mott had to say about his thirteen-year association with the renowned evangelist:

> Beginning with Mount Hermon in 1886, I literally sat at his feet for four weeks. . . . All of us delegates were brought into intimate touch with him, not only listening to his powerful sermons and pungent Bible expositions, but also out under the elms plying him by the hour with our questions. After that I had face-to-face contacts with him at least once every year. . . . I was permitted to see him in action in some of the most notable and fruitful evangelistic campaigns of his wonderful career.[11]

Mott learned from Moody the importance of Christian unity and ecumenical activity. From Moody's concern for the body and soul as expressed in his work with the poor in Chicago, Mott came to believe it unwise to compartmentalize Christian ministries as either spiritual or social. He also learned much from Moody about fundraising and effective communication.

COMMON THREADS

D. L. Moody, Hudson Taylor, and John R. Mott are just three of literally hundreds of profiles of personal growth that I could offer. My passion for world evangelism is reflected in my selection of these historical mentors. If you are to realize your dreams, you will need your own heroes of faith and leadership who ignite passion for your field of service.

As I reflect on these great men and their even greater dreams, I identify five common threads of lifelong learning.

Be Intentional

First, lifelong learners take initiative and accept responsibility for their own growth. Moody was always asking questions, Mott pored over books, and Hudson Taylor sought out information about China immediately upon forming his dream to serve there. Lifelong learners initiate personal growth. Take Mott's advice and "link up your life with a great cause." A burning dream will push you to take initiative.

Be Disciplined

Second, lifelong learners are disciplined in the pursuit of personal growth. Moody and Mott found the early morning hours to be the "choicest time of the day." For you, that choice time may be late at night. The time of day is not what matters; what matters is that you devote regular time to personal growth.

Be Humble

Third, lifelong learners maintain a humble spirit that opens the doorway to growth. Moody was never afraid to say "I don't know" when asked a question by students. He routinely surrounded himself with others who were better educated than himself, and he redeemed every opportunity to learn from them. Mott, though a student at a leading university, was not above sitting at the feet of Moody, who'd had only a few years of formal education. Lifelong learners move beyond the insecurity and defensiveness that comes from pride, opening themselves to learn from anyone.

Be Creative

Fourth, lifelong learners are creative in the pursuit of personal growth. These men created innovative learning opportunities, such as Moody's Question Drawer and Mott's Quiet Day. Hudson Taylor earned the equivalent of a degree in missiology by observing his own failures and those of others, enabling him to chart a new course for China Inland Mission.

Be Active

Fifth, lifelong learners have a strong drive to apply what they learn. Mott, Moody, and Taylor did not consider learning to be merely thinking; for them, learning was connected to doing. When Hudson Taylor learned of ways to better prepare for China, he took action. When Mott learned principles from

Moody, he began to practice them. When Moody saw the power of literature and practical training, he started a publishing house and a school. Although Moody and Mott were at opposite ends of the formal education continuum, they shared a passion for lifelong learning and a commitment to application.

Historical mentors are a powerful source of inspiration that can push you to become all that God intended. Follow their example by taking initiative, remaining disciplined, learning from anyone, and applying what you learn. As you are inspired by your own heroes, your life may become an example for others. Who knows? you might someday become a stepping-stone for younger leaders to follow.

LEVERAGE POINTS

1. Who in your existing network of relationships provides the most powerful model of personal growth? How might you maximize your association with that person to leverage your own growth?

2. Which of the historical mentors mentioned in this chapter was most inspiring to you? Why? What is the most important practical application that you learned from that person's example?

3. If you could choose any historical person to be your mentor for one year, who would it be? What would you like to learn from him or her? Where would you begin?

4. Review the personal growth principles that the three leaders in this chapter had in common (see "Common Threads" on page 73–74). Which of these attributes do you need to work on the most?

PART 2

The Power of Growing

You must grow to realize your dreams.

*Your dream will appear on the horizon, not at arms length.
It is up to you to create the path that will reach it.*

SIX

Focusing Your Energy

Characteristics of a Healthy Growth Plan

If you have made it this far into a book about pursuing your dreams, the chances are good that you are highly motivated to seek personal growth. But motivation is not enough. Highly motivated people can engage in counterproductive, even self-destructive, behavior in pursuit of their goals. Unbridled desire, the raw expression of motivation, actually increases your vulnerability to counterproductive behavior.

Think of the people who want to get out of debt so bad that they spend half of their paycheck on lottery tickets. How about those so desperate to make a relationship work that they drive their partners away by their controlling behavior? The motivation to achieve a better life is present in each case; but unaccompanied by good decision making and healthy behavior, it produces disastrous results. Motivation without direction is a recipe for ruin. In the words of Solomon, Israel's wisest king, "It is not good to have zeal without knowledge, nor to be hasty and miss the way."[1] There is such a thing as unhealthy growth planning.

In high school, I was not a motivated learner. I'm not proud of it, but for most of my four years, I was a classic underachiever. It was probably the season of my life with the highest P/A Differential. And my D/A Differential was zero—not because I had a highly developed capacity but because I had no dream. I naïvely assumed that the Cs on my report card resulted only from my failure to show up consistently for class or pay attention when I did. I thought that if I ever discovered a reason to learn, I could get better grades.

After high school, I worked as a truck driver for a lumberyard in my hometown. That was a positive learning experience: I learned that I would not be fulfilled very long in that line of work! I gained a new desire—a dream—to go to college. I decided to pursue a childhood interest and study radiologic technology with an emphasis on CT scanning. But in a matter of weeks after enrolling in college, I realized that motivation alone would not position me to excel. I had to undo the negative patterns I had developed in high school and break out of a cycle of counterproductive behavior. I needed to learn how to learn.

The studying I did in high school would more accurately be described as cramming. In the shortest time possible, I stuffed the minimum number of facts, terms, dates—whatever was needed—into my brain. Then I would hurry to class, hoping the answers would fall into the right places on the test. My method was all short cuts; my grades revealed how ineffective that system was.

Looking back, I see how that first semester opened my mind to a life-stage dream of graduating from college and pursuing a meaningful career. The emergence of a dream both generated and exposed my capacity challenge. Suddenly, I knew what I didn't know: how to study. This D/A Differential generated plenty of motivation, but that would have been insufficient without a change in behavior. I needed a framework and methodology for learning.

So do you. If you are to grow in any area of life, you must first determine how you will learn. You need a viable plan for growth. Here are the basics of a healthy personal growth plan. This is not a cut-and-paste model that fits every situation; it is a set of principles that you can use to create a unique plan for your personal growth.

REFLECTING YOUR UNIQUENESS

First, a healthy growth plan reflects your uniqueness as a person. It makes sense that a *personal* growth plan begins with you, but that is not as simple as it seems. For many people, the spark that ignites a desire to grow is the glaring difference between their capacity and that of those around them. Are you quick to notice how much better other people are at performing various tasks than you are? That's discouraging, isn't it? It is also irrelevant, since *your* capacity needs to be directed at *your* dreams, not theirs. The lion's share of your capacity challenge is dream-specific.

Sir Edmund Hillary dreamed of standing atop Mount Everest. After participating in two reconnaissance missions for climbers who then failed to reach the summit, Hillary shook his fist at the mountain and declared, "I'll defeat you yet, because you are as big as you are going to get but I'm still growing." The determined New Zealander kept sharpening his strategy and refining his skills as a mountaineer, and the long, arduous process finally paid off. At 11:30 a.m. on May 29, 1953, Sir Edmund Hillary and his guide, Tenzing Norgay, stood on the rooftop of the world at 29,028 feet above sea level. Hillary grew in order to realize his dream.

I'm inspired by Sir Edmund's example, and I, too, love awe-inspiring mountains. I've been to the Andes, the Himalayas, and the Alps, and I live in the shadow of the Rockies. But I'm never going to be a mountaineer. Sir Edmund's dream is not mine. I have my own capacity challenge.

It requires a high level of self-awareness to focus on your uniqueness. This self-awareness comes more naturally for some than others. Consider these six components of what I call your *Identity Profile*: Personality, Passion, Talents, Skills, Spiritual Gifts,[2] and Dreams. A healthy growth plan flows from the uniqueness of your identity—the essence of who God created you to be. Each component of your Identity Profile represents one aspect of your capacity, and you should examine each component under the spotlight of personal growth. (You'll learn how to do that in chapter 8.) The self-awareness that you will gain from this activity results in a healthy self-confidence that is expressed in the prayer of Danish theologian Søren Kierkegaard, who said, "And now Lord, with your help, I shall become myself."

BUILDING ON STRENGTHS

Second, a healthy personal growth plan builds on your strengths. There is probably no more pervasive myth about personal growth than the notion that it should major on weaknesses instead of strengths. Focusing on your strengths is counterintuitive, but building on your weaknesses is counterproductive.

Most of us could list our top five weaknesses with minimal effort. But imagine trying to name them in the presence of your closest friends, those who know you best. Can you picture it? The slightest pause on your part would probably bring a chorus of fill-in-the-blanks, which may be why you are so focused on your shortcomings in the first place. It seems only natural to give attention to areas of weakness if you want to reduce your D/A Differential. But—watch this closely—majoring on your weaknesses is a denial of who you are, of who God made you to be, and it is an obstacle to your personal growth.

The Gallup organization has researched this subject, interviewing more than two million people. The results formed the basis for the book *Now, Discover Your Strengths* by Marcus Buckingham and Donald Clifton. Persuasive neurological findings indicate that your natural talents are hardwired into your nervous system by the handiwork of God.[3] You are who you are—with certain talents and an inclination toward learning in given areas—because God made you that way.

Buckingham and Clifton go on to emphasize that *talents* become *strengths* when the right knowledge and skills are added to them.[4] That means you will never develop the consistent, near-perfect performance of a strength if you do not have natural talent underlying your knowledge and skill. Therefore, shoring up weaknesses is merely a survival tactic and not a developmental priority. You must manage weaknesses in order to keep from falling short in critical areas of responsibility, but never squander mental energy or time trying to turn a weakness into a strength. It can't be done. Healthy growth planning focuses energy on areas where you can create the powerful combination of talent, knowledge, and skill to develop a true strength.

There is one notable exception to strength-based developmental focus: character weaknesses. Heart-level deficits in character and integrity are always a cause for concern. It would *never* be justifiable to say, "I'm sorry, but self-control is not one of my strengths. I don't waste time working it." Everyone can improve in the area of character—this is not a matter of talent. You must give appropriate energy to correcting any weaknesses in your character.

HOLISTIC

Third, a healthy personal growth plan is holistic, encompassing all of life. I view life as a complex and interconnected whole with no practical distinction between the sacred and the secular. Yet I have found it helpful to identify five *life domains* (or *roles*) that are common to everyone: personal, family, Kingdom, vocation, and community.[5]

Your personal life domain reflects the physical, emotional, social, mental, and spiritual aspects of your well-being. Your family life domain is the set of relationships that includes your family and other inner-circle confidants. The domain of your vocation includes your work and everything connected to it. Your Kingdom domain is your involvement with and service to a place of worship. The community domain is your connection to neighborhood or city, including everything from your relationships with your neighbors to volunteer service as a Little League coach or crisis pregnancy counselor.

Since your primary motivation for growth comes from your dream, it is common for your growth planning to focus on one or two life domains. For driven, career-oriented people like me, those domains are typically personal (with an emphasis on giftedness) and vocation. But most people have more than one dream: we envision possibilities also for our families, communities, and churches. While your growth plan may focus on one or two domains, it must include all of them.

If you need an incentive to take a holistic approach to growth, consider this encouragement and the warning that follows it. A balanced life—a stable family, vibrant spirituality, and healthy community involvement—significantly supports the pursuit of vocational dreams. But here is a warning: cutting corners in the life domains that don't seem directly related to career goals often exacts a severe price in the form of broken relationships and lasting regrets.

Jack Coleman enjoyed success as president of Haverford College, professor at Massachusetts Institute of Technology, and chair of the Federal Reserve Bank of Philadelphia. Yet he expressed remorse for his lack of balanced growth, saying, "One of my greatest sorrows I will carry to my dying day is that I never saw my youngest son on the stage [when] he was at a private school, the Westown School. I don't think it's twenty minutes away from the Haverford campus. I never saw him. I was too busy. And I'm going to regret that forever."[6]

Healthy growth planning is holistic, acknowledging the interconnectedness of life and supporting a diverse set of dreams.

MOTIVATED BY STEWARDSHIP

Fourth, a healthy personal growth plan is motivated by a sense of stewardship, the desire to add value to others and bring glory to God. There is nothing inherently wrong with the desire to achieve, succeed, or be rewarded, but the motivation for doing so matters. Like an unchecked infection in the body, impure motives can destroy a dream. And infection can enter through the smallest of sores.

When your capacity challenge is driven by a God-inspired dream, it will generate pure, unselfish, altruistic motives. These motives flow from the sacred trust inherited by each of us by virtue of our creation in the image of God. We are endowed with God-given resources and dreams, and we are responsible to God for the way we use them. That concept is known as *stewardship*. In some of His parables, Jesus taught that we will be held accountable for our stewardship in life, not based on how we did in comparison to others but on what we did with the inner resources God has given to us.[7] It is clear from these parables that God expects each of us to develop our capacity in pursuit of His dreams and in service to others.

In God's economy, the end does not justify the means. You may rationalize the need to take shortcuts now based on the good they will enable you to do later, but you are fooling only yourself. You are accountable for the manner in which you live. When you least expect it, the curtain will fall, exposing the props and gadgets that have been hidden there all along.

A vignette from the movie *The Emperor's Club* powerfully illustrates the futility of cutting corners. In the film, Kevin Kline plays William Hundert, a career teacher of privileged boys at St. Benedict's school. The school's annual Mister Julius Ceasar contest is a demanding test of Roman history, Hundert's subject. The last boy standing wins the equivalent of the school's MVP award for the year and joins an elite group of intellectual giants whose names forever adorn its hallowed halls. One student, Sedgwick Bell, is a newcomer and the son of a senator; Hundert takes a special interest in helping young Bell fit in. But he is more interested in finding ways to break the rules than in developing his capacity.

After Bell shows some flashes of genius, Hundert catches him cheating in the Mister Julius Caesar competition. What makes matters worse is that Hundert, based on his desire to give Bell a start, had given him a slot in the contest that should have gone to another boy whose classroom performance was better. Honoring the wishes of the headmaster, Hundert does not expose Bell's dishonesty.

Years later Hundert is invited by Bell, all expenses paid, to a class reunion at a posh Long Island resort. The grown-up Sedgwick Bell has initiated the reunion to recreate the Mister Julius Ceasar contest and regain his honor—against the same contestants to whom he had lost by cheating years ago. Hundert asks the questions, and in the dramatic waning moments of the contest, discovers that Bell is cheating once again. Adding irony to the story, part of Bell's agenda for the reunion is to announce his run for the Senate on a platform of reestablishing the nation's moral and fiscal leadership.

Hundert eventually confronts his erstwhile student, in the men's room, about his dishonesty in the competition. There the teacher offers this final lecture: "All of us, at some point, are forced to look at ourselves in the mirror and see who we really are. And when that day comes for you Sedgwick, you will be confronted with a life lived without virtue and without principle. For that I pity you. End of lesson."

Bell responds: "I live in the real world, where people do what they need to do to get what they want. If it's lying, if it's cheating, then so be it. So I am going to go out there and I am going to win that election, Mr. Hundert. And you will see me everywhere. And I will worry about my contribution later."

The dialogue is punctuated by the flush of a toilet. As Hundert and Bell turn to leave, the door to a bathroom stall creaks open. To Bell's surprise, his preteen son emerges. He has heard the entire conversation, and his face can't begin to conceal his sadness and disbelief. Ignoring his father's repeated calls, the boy turns his back and walks away, leaving Sedgwick Bell to wrestle with the Machiavellian philosophy that poisons his life.

In the pursuit of your dreams, the *why* and the *how* are as important as the *what*.

AGGRESSIVE AND REALISTIC

Fifth, a healthy personal growth plan is both aggressive and realistic. There is a fine line between stretching beyond your comfort zone and stretching so far that you become discouraged. A healthy plan straddles that line, pushing you to the edge without generating the loop of negative feedback caused by chronic failure and disappointment.

Ideally, your growth plan will have goals that span the spectrum of difficulty. Making progress in areas that are strategic but less difficult builds momentum for reaching goals that push the limits of your ability. It's important to gain outside perspectives as you walk this tightrope. Seek the input of peers or mentors to reality-test your personal growth goals.

Specific, Measurable, and Written

Sixth, a healthy personal growth plan is specific, measurable, and written. There is no value in setting goals if you can't tell when or if you have reached them. Vague goals deny the sense of closure and accomplishment that comes from fulfilling them. Pursuing ill-defined goals is like being in a race with no finish line.

Healthy growth plans include well-defined goals that articulate either specific outcomes or specific activities and how you will recognize their completion. Putting your goals on paper is a powerful exercise in personal accountability. Defining in writing how you plan to grow is like shooting the starter's pistol at the beginning of a race. Sharing that written plan with others is like adding a cheering crowd along the course; it provides inspiration and affirmation as you head for the finish line.

In chapter 11, you will learn how to use a Growth Planning Summary Sheet, which provides a simple framework for recording the key elements of each goal. Using this simple form will ensure that each of your goals is specific, measurable, and written.

Time Bound and Habit Forming

Finally, a healthy personal growth plan is both time bound and habit forming. Your growth plan will have a starting date and an ending date—it will be time bound. Of course, many of the goals you identify in your growth plan represent practices you'll want to continue well beyond the scope of a specific growth cycle.

As you continue these practices, you create *growth habits* that will drive ongoing change in your life. Aristotle said, "We are what we repeatedly do.

Excellence, then, is not an act, but a habit." Completing your growth goals can bring exponential benefits when they move from being stand-alone projects to being positive habits, woven into the fabric of your life. Even modest improvements, repeated again and again, can make a dramatic difference. The margin between average and excellent can be very small, and what seems like a nominal gain can become a strategic advantage when extrapolated over time.

Baseball is an example of this principle. If you hit safely 270 times in 1,000 plate appearances, you would be an average player. If you could increase your success rate to 320 hits per 1,000 at bats—and sustain that performance over a number of years—you would be a first-ballot Hall of Fame player. Since the average player gets about 500 plate appearances per year, a so-so player and a superstar are separated by only about 25 hits per season over a career.

Motivation for growth is important, but you will need more than motivation to keep growing. You will need a framework or system that harnesses your inner drive, channeling every ounce of energy in a positive direction. Think of these growth-plan characteristics as the banks of your river, and be careful to stay within them. In the next chapter we'll discover how to not only stay within the banks but also increase the flow and create real momentum for your personal growth.

LEVERAGE POINTS

1. Make a list of at least five personal growth goals you have pursued in the last few years. Which of them focused on weaknesses instead of strengths? How did this affect your progress?

2. Review the life domains listed on page 83. How many of these domains are represented in the five goals you listed in the question above? What areas need to be added or emphasized in your growth planning?

3. If you were asked to produce a written overview of your current personal growth goals, could you do it? If you have not written your goals, how seriously do you take them?

4. Your dreams may be either self-inspired or God-inspired. How would you characterize the relationship between the source of a dream and the purity of the motives that drive it? What is the origin of your current dreams? What are your current motives for pursuing personal growth?

SEVEN

Generating Momentum

A Repeatable Cycle for Personal Growth

W hen our children were younger, my wife and I liked to track their physical growth by marking their height on the wall in our kitchen. We didn't line them up every morning to see how much they'd grown overnight, but over longer periods of time, those rising pencil marks made it easy to see why they needed new clothes all the time. They were growing.

The normal growth rate for a child is about two-and-a-half inches per year from age two until puberty. Upon reaching puberty, a teenager's body releases powerful hormones that trigger a myriad of rapid changes in physical growth, sexual maturation, and physiological development. No wonder we associate fear and anxiety with rapid change!

I have often wondered what it would be like if there were a mental or spiritual equivalent to the hormone storm that triggers rapid development in a teenager. Can you imagine finding a way to generate bursts of personal growth that would accelerate your progress toward realizing your dreams?

In fact there are ways to generate momentum for personal growth. Throughout your life, you will encounter opportunities for spontaneous growth. As you learn to identify and capitalize on these naturally occurring growth triggers, you will experience growth spurts in your personal life.

You can sustain the momentum produced by these spontaneous growth spurts by developing an intentional cycle of personal growth.

SPONTANEOUS GROWTH TRIGGERS

As I review my own personal growth over the years, I can see that outside sources triggered most of my rapid growth. Although the motivation for growth is primarily internal, the stimulation for growth is usually external. Spontaneous growth triggers come in a variety of forms. All of them are naturally recurring phenomena that we encounter, such as challenging opportunities and new relationships. Everyone encounters spontaneous growth triggers. The question is, how will you respond to them?

As you become more aware of possible growth triggers, you can begin turning these ordinary situations into on-ramps to the fast lane of personal learning. Here is my list of growth triggers; you may be able to name a few more. Most important is that you begin to identify the experiences that can stimulate rapid personal growth.

Difficult or Important Questions

Difficult, probing, or important questions can open doorways to profound learning and personal growth. I began an annual exercise, which has become one of my most important personal growth tools, because of a challenging question asked on an exam by a college professor. We had been studying the lives of great leaders in history, people who were world changers in their day. First, I was asked to make a list of five world changers from among the people we had been studying and identify the common traits that might explain how they made such a lasting contribution. In other words, I was asked to say what made them world changers.

Then came the question that really captured my imagination: "Identify the five most important traits you will need to cultivate to become a world changer." I still remember the quiet but life-changing moment when I realized that my professor actually believed I could become a world changer. I thought to myself, *This question accounts for a full 20 percent of my grade on this test. He really believes God could use me to change the world.*

Since that day, I have studied the lives of great leaders in a process I call historical mentoring. Every year I pick a new mentor from history and learn from that person by reading his or her biography. I am hungry to apply what I learn from these historical mentors and eager for God to use me in a similar way. This asset to my lifelong growth came unexpectedly by means of an exam question. You will frequently be faced with challenging or difficult questions that press you to observe the world or to acquire knowledge. Use those questions as triggers for personal growth.

Challenging Opportunities

Circumstances that push us out of our comfort zone can also be springboards to personal growth. Six months after graduating from college, I led a team of people to Liberia, West Africa, where we conducted programs for children and youth, and held meetings in churches. I expected to speak in only about three or four church services because several other team members wanted the opportunity to speak as well.

Upon our arrival, we discovered that our itinerary had been expanded. Many more services had been added to our trip. In addition, all but one of the team members got cold feet when it came to speaking in front of a group. I was now faced with the challenge of speaking seventeen times in twenty-one days! Being only six months out of college, I didn't have seventeen messages even back home in my office, let alone in my briefcase. And our schedule was jammed, leaving very limited time for preparation.

This challenging opportunity forced me into a hurry-up growth mode. Two things became immediately apparent: I desperately needed divine help in order to be effective, and I had to learn to speak from an outline rather than from a full manuscript. I made adjustments immediately, relying on God to give direction to my preparation time and forcing myself to work from an outline. That subtle change gave me greater freedom while speaking, allowing me to move around on the platform and become more conversational in my delivery. I grew more as a communicator during those three weeks than I had during the previous three years combined.

New Experiences

Nearly every exposure to a new idea or experience presents an opportunity for personal growth. The life of Cameron Townsend provides one of my favorite examples. As a twenty-three-year-old leader, "Cam" Townsend served as a missionary in Guatemala. As he distributed Bibles from village to village, he realized that many of Guatemala's Indians did not speak Spanish. One day an Indian asked him, "If your God is so smart, why can't he speak our language?"

Instead of seeing the experience as a roadblock, Townsend saw it as a trigger for personal growth. He learned the Cakchiquel language and translated the New Testament into it. He then turned his attention to the languages of other tribes. Spurred on by this experience, Townsend eventually founded Wycliffe Bible Translators and its sister organization, Summer Institute of Linguistics.

Stimulating Relationships

Relationships are often the gateway to new experiences and challenging opportunities. You don't need a stereotypically sanguine personality to benefit from stimulating relationships. Everyone, regardless of temperament, can be alert for relational connections that trigger personal growth.

An important key to making use of this spontaneous growth trigger is to cultivate true charisma. Truly charismatic people are focused on others. When they enter a room or encounter new people, they don't fixate on themselves by asking insecure questions such as *Do I look okay?* or *Will anyone here be interested in me?* Instead, they focus on other people and what can be learned from them, which often helps to reduce the insecurity level of everyone in the room.[1]

A few years ago, my wife, Sherry, invited a couple to our house for dinner. Sherry had gotten to know these folk through her responsibilities at a charter school in our community that she had helped to start. Over dinner, I consciously engaged our guests in conversation, seeking to learn more about them and from them. I discovered that our new friend Leslie had considerable experience as an educator with an emphasis in individual learning styles. As I showed genuine interest and a desire to learn, it became apparent that she loved her work and enjoyed talking about it.

I learned that Leslie had just attended a Gallup workshop on strengths-based learning. She described an assessment tool that I knew would have significant implications for personal growth planning. I jotted down some key ideas along with the name of the book *Now, Discover Your Strengths*, which I refer to in the previous chapter. Before our friends' car was fully out of the driveway, I was at my computer ordering the book online. I summarized several pages of the material to share with my friends at Top Flight Leadership, and they have incorporated it into their team and have enlisted Gallup-approved trainers for EuroTrain, their flagship training experience for young leaders.

I have seen Leslie only a few times since the night she and her husband visited our home, but for the rest of my life, I will benefit from that encounter. Why? Not because I met a new person, but because I chose to engage that person with an "others" focus and a sincere desire to learn. An ancient bit of wisdom holds that "as iron sharpens iron, so one man sharpens another."[2] Whenever you are around knowledgeable, interesting people, probe them with questions about their experiences, what they are reading, and what new dreams they are processing. As you do, you will trip spontaneous triggers for your own personal growth.

Paradigm Shifts

We have one of the greatest of all learning opportunities when we experience a paradigm shift. A paradigm shift is a radical change in perspective, usually arising from a challenge to previously held assumptions or beliefs. This shift in thinking results in new combinations, different working models, and all kinds of outside-the-box thinking that had not been previously considered.

Once you have made a paradigm shift, it can be hard to believe that your present perspective was once a radically new way of thinking. The theories of Copernicus are an example of this. In direct opposition to the teachings of Aristotle and the second-century astronomer Ptolemy, Copernicus theorized that the earth revolved around the sun. His ideas were so controversial and demanded such a radical paradigm shift that his book *On the Revolutions of the Heavenly Spheres* was published with this anonymous foreword: "The theory put forward in this book is only a mathematical hypothesis . . . cosmological interpretations are reserved for the philosophers."

After Copernicus's death, his ideas were reinforced by Newton's law of universal gravitation, and what had been viewed as a radical perspective on the solar system slowly became accepted as fact. They are now the bedrock of astronomical teaching. The paradigm shift was complete. Today it is difficult to think of the idea that the earth revolves around the sun as a new concept. Most of us will experience only a handful of paradigm shifts in our lifetime. But when they occur, they present us with a rare personal growth trigger.

I recently spoke with someone who suggested that within my lifetime, it will be possible to travel from one place to another in a manner similar to that depicted by the transporters on the television series *Star Trek*. You may be chuckling right now, recalling Captain Kirk's famous line, "Beam me up, Scotty." The reason you're rolling your eyes over that possibility is that it requires a paradigm shift, a radical new way of interpreting reality. Who knows whether this form of travel will ever happen? But if it does, it won't take long for those who use it to look back at us and snicker in the same way we do at those who scoffed at Copernicus. Some of the most important learning adventures of your lifetime will require you to see things differently—very differently. That is why you need to be alert for the possibility of a paradigm shift.

Personal Failure

Perhaps the one universally available growth trigger is personal failure. Everyone experiences failure at one time or another. Yet from the ashes of disappointment, many learners have rekindled a flame of personal growth that lit the way to success.

The great British statesman Winston Churchill tasted his share of failure, eventually defining success as "moving from failure to failure without loss of enthusiasm." As a young leader, Churchill refined his public speaking abilities while campaigning for public office. He became adept at giving several speeches on a wide variety of subjects in a single night. He lost in his initial run for office, but he built on the experience, eventually winning a seat in Parliament. At age twenty-nine, while giving a speech to the House of Commons, Churchill lost his train of thought in mid-sentence. He stopped, appeared confused, and sat down mumbling, "I thank the honorable Members for having listened to me." From that day on, he ceased relying on memorized or spontaneous speeches and supplemented his copious memory with a full manuscript. Failure became a fertile breeding ground for personal growth, leading him to craft powerful speeches that would galvanize the Allies against the evils of Nazism. Reflect on this short list of spontaneous growth triggers:

- Difficult or important questions

- Challenging opportunities

- New experiences

- Stimulating relationships

- Paradigm shifts

- Personal failure

Most of us encounter at least one of these potential growth triggers every week of our lives. Now imagine what your growth chart would look like if you turned these opportunities into an upward spiral of personal development. It is certain that you will encounter personal growth triggers. What will you do with them?

Intentional Growth Cycles

Spontaneous growth triggers do not, by themselves, lead to lifelong learning. In fact, personal growth spurts have lasting value only within the context of an intentional growth cycle. Once you have determined that you must grow in order to realize your dreams, you will need to create a cycle of personal growth—a pattern that can be repeated again and again.

A *growth cycle* is a framework for planning, managing, and tracking your personal development. A growth cycle is to an individual what a fiscal year is to an organization. Many companies choose a starting and stopping point for their fiscal year that matches their business cycle, not the calendar. This fiscal year provides a logical framework for managing their annual financial records. The company's reports, financial audits, and other important business must be completed at the end of its fiscal cycle, which occurs on the same date every year.

In much the same way, you need to establish a personal growth cycle, a fixed, repeatable, period of time within which you will accomplish certain personal growth goals. At the end of your growth cycle, you can conduct a *growth audit*, reviewing how you did the previous year. Based on that audit, you can develop a *growth budget*, a new set of goals for the following cycle.

Don't make the common mistake of not taking growth cycles seriously. Of all the people I have coached in growth planning, the only ones who have demonstrated staying power were those who have made it a priority to create a personal growth cycle for themselves. By doing so, they moved seamlessly from one growth plan into the next with little or no loss of momentum. In contrast, one of the clearest common denominators I have seen in those who fell off the personal growth planning wagon is the failure to develop a personal growth cycle.

Unlike fiscal years, personal growth cycles do not have to be 365 days in length. But most people do gravitate toward a one-year time frame. Here are a few hints for establishing a growth cycle.

Build on Natural Momentum

First, choose a season of the year to begin your cycle that takes advantage of your natural momentum. You have an intuitive awareness of when you are most productive during the course of an average day or week. When asked if you are a morning person or a night owl, you are likely to answer immediately. You probably have a weekly work rhythm as well. Some people move into the week with lots of energy and want to tackle their most important project on Monday. Others recognize their need to pick up speed and prefer to hold major tasks for Tuesday or Wednesday.

A personal growth cycle applies this same sense of natural momentum to the larger context of a quarter or even a year. Some people find the New Year to be the best time to initiate a personal growth plan. Others find that the back-to-school routine of fall provides an ideal framework to refocus on growth. People who live in a colder climate with clearly defined seasonal changes may find the greening of spring to be a stimulus for personal development. Still others prefer the relaxed pace of summer with its weeks of vacation is the best time to initiate planned self-improvement. When establishing a personal growth cycle, ask yourself, "How can I capitalize on the natural momentum that flows from my seasonal rhythms?"

A simple way to get started with this process is to take a piece of scrap paper and draw a simple timeline for one year, marking the four quarters numerically. Begin by making winter the first quarter. Then reflect on your year, considering your natural momentum and recurring events such as an annual trade show at work, summer vacation, or your child's Little League baseball season. Once you have plotted the major landmarks of your typical year, consider how it would affect your personal growth momentum to begin or end your cycle in each season. Begin with winter, and consider beginning your cycle in each season of the year. This exercise may appear superficial at first glance, but it is worthy of unhurried, reflective thinking. Eventually, you will discover the season, perhaps even the month or week, that will best serve as the beginning of your growth year.

My own growth cycle begins and ends in March. For me, spring is an invigorating season in which to begin, and the final quarter (January through March) gets a natural boost of momentum from the winter holidays and the excitement of starting a new calendar year. Summer is my least productive time for personal growth due to work-related international travel and a vacation schedule that still includes younger children. Remember, effective growth planning reflects your uniqueness as a person. You need to settle on a cycle that works best in your circumstances. Beginning at the right time will position you for seamless transitions from one growth plan to the next over the rest of your life.

Select a Meaningful Start Date

Just as a corporate fiscal year is started on a particular day of the calendar year, your growth cycle needs to begin on a specific day, not just within a given season. Once you have settled on a season that fits your natural momentum, select a start date that has some personal significance.

I prefer a one-year cycle since my growth plan often includes several extensive goals that require longer blocks of time to complete. I also find that it gives me room to embrace spontaneous growth opportunities—those outside of my plan—without feeling pressure that I'll get behind schedule on my planned growth goals. My birthday is March 14 and is a natural choice for the start date of my growth cycle—partly because I share that birthday with my dad. I was born on his twenty-fifth birthday.

As you choose your annual start date, look for significant, life-shaping experiences that occurred in the season you have selected as the first quarter of your growth cycle. It could be something memorable, such as the date your high school team won the championship or the date you met your spouse. You might choose a date associated with a favorite historical mentor, such as the day he or she was born, died, or accomplished something noteworthy. Choose any date you like, but do choose one, the more meaningful the better.

Plan an Anniversary Event

Mark the completion of your growth cycle with an annual event held on or near your start date. Consider this event a personal growth retreat, even if you don't go out of town or stay overnight. This celebration will create a bookend for your annual developmental journey and will formalize your starting and ending point. As an ending point, it will be like the tape at the finish line of a race. As it comes into view, it will spur an extra burst of energy and help you finish strong. The starting aspect of your retreat will be like the starter's pistol, causing you to leap from the blocks to begin the new cycle.

My annual closure-and-kickoff event has become one of the most meaningful components of my growth cycle. It is a high point of my year, something I cannot imagine doing without. This event revolves around a meeting with my dad, who is a primary life mentor to me. I've even given our meeting a name. I call it a destiny checkup. Dad and I try to meet as close to our birthday as possible, holing up in a hotel for twenty-four hours. We spend time reflecting on the prior year and sharing the goals we have mapped out for the next twelve months.

I am very fortunate to have this kind of interaction with someone else, namely my father. But regardless of your circumstances, you can plan a productive event that will become a benchmark in your personal growth cycle. Consider these suggestions.

Block Off a Full Day. Schedule the better part of a full day—at least eight hours, twenty-four if possible—because you don't want to rush this process. You will want enough time to work through your agenda and still take a walk now and then to clear your mind or just get the circulation flowing. I have never come away from a destiny checkup with the feeling that twenty-four hours was too long a time to spend.

Get Away. Go somewhere that will separate you from the daily pressures of life. You don't have to travel across the country to break your routine; a private study room at the public library may be all you need. The point is to get some emotional space and find a place to unhook from the daily grind so you can focus your thoughts on plans for growing toward your life dreams.

Prepare Well. Maximize your retreat time by preparing well. Be sure to bring along your growth audit (evaluation of the previous cycle's goals) and your growth budget (the roadmap for next year's growth plan). It's important to understand that the purpose of this event is *not* to create your growth audit and budget. It is to review your completed audit and to present (not prepare) a new personal growth budget. You will need to spend time over the weeks prior to your annual event evaluating the previous year and planning for the next cycle. I do whatever it takes to ensure that I show up for my destiny checkup with documents in hand, ready to maximize the time I will have with my father, which brings me to the next suggestion.

Include Another Person. Involve another person for some or all of your closure and kickoff special event. Whether it is a peer or a mentor, be sure that the person knows you well, cares deeply about you reaching your dreams, and brings some objectivity to the table. Even if you choose to spend most of your day alone, consider adding a telephone meeting to the event. You will benefit greatly from sharing your journey with a growth partner.

People often ask for more details about what my dad and I actually do during our annual destiny checkup. Perhaps an inside look at our schedule will stimulate some creative thinking on your part. Dad and I typically convene around dinnertime and connect over a leisurely meal. Since we live about two thousand miles apart, the first hour or so is usually a time for small talk and relational catch-up. After dinner, we spend some time in prayer, thanking God for another year and asking for His wisdom.

We continue by sharing our top-ten list of books from the previous year, regardless of whether we read them as a formal part of our personal growth plans or not. My dad has powerfully modeled for me the importance of reading as a source of learning. In preparation for one of our first destiny checkups, he struggled to create a list of the top ten books he had read; it was very difficult for him to select only ten of the nearly seventy-five books he had read that year. I promised not to be too hard on him.

We call our time a destiny checkup because it includes a reflective analysis of my written life purpose. After reviewing our year's reading, I share thoughts related to my life dreams, and we look at how I am progressing toward the stated list of ultimate contributions by which I hope to be remembered.

We often end our evening with a serious review of the NCAA basketball tournament pairings. We meet during "March Madness" and take advantage of our common love for sports as a healthy break from the intensity of personal growth interaction. The closure/kickoff event doesn't need to be all business.

The next morning we review my written report from the previous year's growth goals. We then give similar attention to the personal growth summary sheets I have created for the next cycle. We wrap up our time by sharing prayer requests and giving our final few hours to once again seeking God's wisdom.

You have tremendous latitude in planning your own annual growth event. A good pattern for your event is any design that you can follow repeatedly to get the same results. You will create momentum by capitalizing on events or experiences that trigger personal growth spurts. You will retain that momentum by creating a personal growth cycle that you can repeat again and again.

TURNING THE CORNER

By now you have evaluated your Capacity Index and have some idea of your D/A Differential. You have spent time processing your dreams, seeking to leverage your capacity, believability, opportunity, and legacy challenges as ongoing sources of motivation. You have taken a serious look at reducing the restraining forces that pose barriers to your personal growth. You have reassessed your understanding of personal development in light of the characteristics of a healthy growth plan, and you have established a personal growth cycle, complete with a start date and an annual event for kickoff and closure.

Now it's time to turn the corner and get even more practical, taking an in-depth look at how to grow on purpose. You know that if you are to realize your dreams, you will need to grow. The next four chapters will show you how.

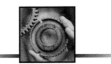

LEVERAGE POINTS

1. Think back over the last week and make a list of difficult questions, challenging opportunities, new experiences, stimulating relationships, and personal failures that you encountered. How effective were you at turning those experiences into personal growth triggers?

2. Review the steps in creating a personal growth cycle on pages 95–100. Identify your personal growth cycle, including both a season and specific date.

3. Develop a plan for a kickoff-and-closure event, including a tentative schedule and the names of those whom you will include in the event.

EIGHT

Taking Inventory

Doing a Personal Growth Assessment

I f you have ever worked in a retail environment, you are familiar with the routine of taking inventory. Even as a customer, you have probably encountered the inventory process while stumbling through a store aisle that was more like an obstacle course than a customer-friendly display of goods. Nobody likes taking inventory. It's a cumbersome process that involves counting every item in the store to create an accurate register of the store's merchandise. But inventory is a necessary business practice. Without it, managers never have an accurate picture of what's in stock. Although it requires a time-consuming process, every successful business takes inventory at least once each year.

Doing a personal growth assessment is a lot like taking inventory at a store. Done properly, a personal assessment will guide you systematically down the aisles of your life, causing you to give attention to the contents of every shelf. When you're finished, you'll know exactly "what's in stock" in your life spiritually, personally, and professionally. A growth assessment adds detail to the snapshot provided by your Capacity Index; it shows exactly where you need to grow. If you are serious about personal growth, you will engage in a process of self-assessment at least once a year.

CULTIVATING SELF-AWARENESS

The term *assessment* sounds technical, and some aspects of a growth assessment are. You will want to use some external tools to help you assess yourself thoroughly. But there is an underlying, internal aspect to self-assessment that is far more valuable than any resource you could purchase. Effective self-assessment hinges on *self-awareness*. You cannot assess what you do not see. Before you can effectively assess yourself, you must cultivate a high level of self-awareness.

The first level of self-awareness is being honest about yourself *with yourself*. The second is being honest about yourself *with others*. Both levels are essential, and they are sequential. You cannot move to the second if have skipped the first. The hallmark of self-awareness is a deep understanding of your emotions, strengths, limitations, values, and motives.[1] This requires a high-octane mixture of honesty and humility. A watered-down view of reality simply will not do. The cultivation of true self-awareness requires self-confidence and personal security reinforced by a grace-awakened, high-trust environment.

The Awareness Gap

It may be easier to recognize the importance of self-awareness by observing the lack of it in people around us. We all have experienced the frustration of trying to relate to someone who is clueless about how obnoxious he is in the eyes of other people. The awkwardness we feel in this kind of relationship is directly proportional to that gap in awareness—the difference between what we know about the person and what he knows about himself.

For example, if I were to make a presentation to your team and begin by making some offhand comments that were insulting to some of those present, your teammates would feel awkward. The emotional tension in the room would stem not from the comments themselves but from the emotional gap that they revealed—the audience would know something about me that I didn't know myself. Suppose someone found a way to graciously point out that I had unwittingly offended some group members. Then I would have a choice to make. I could accept this knowledge about myself and alter my behavior, or I could choose to ignore the information and continue being boorish. You've probably seen examples of people who responded in either way.

Your willingness to change and your ability to focus on the right goals—the twin hinges of personal growth—swing on the level of self-awareness you possess. Self-awareness enables you to accurately answer the critical questions that flow from the Capacity Index: What will you do about your P/A Differential? And what will you do about your D/A Differential? Trying to do a meaningful self-assessment without self-awareness is like looking in a distortion mirror at a carnival; whatever good feeling a five-foot-tall man gains from appearing seven feet tall vanishes the moment he turns to face his six-foot-tall wife. If you do not see yourself accurately, you will never make progress toward your dreams.

Remember, not all awareness gaps are equally important. It's one thing to waltz out of a restaurant with ketchup on your face, but it's quite a different thing to believe you have the capacity to realize your dreams when, in fact, you do not. The true size of your D/A Differential can be masked by an awareness gap. Often, those who care about you will feel a benevolent awkwardness when they see what you don't. They may try to help by pointing out the true level of your actual capacity. If you respond to their help with defensiveness and denial, your believability challenge will expand exponentially. You can share your dream with others all you like, but if you are not fully aware of your D/A Differential, they will never join you. It is crucial that you gain an accurate picture of yourself.

Limiting Factors

The factors that limit self-awareness form a continuum ranging from ignorance (I don't know) to confusion (I'm mistaken) to denial (I refuse to accept the truth). If my lack of self-awareness is caused by ignorance, I need information. If it is caused by confusion, I need clarification. If it is caused by denial, I need confrontation.

When information exposes the ignorance that has limited my self-awareness, I have a choice. I can accept what I have learned about myself, close my awareness gap, and position myself for strategic growth; or I can contest the information and move to the right on the continuum—toward confusion or denial. If I am confused about what I have learned, I have another choice. I can seek clarification and move toward increased self-awareness, or I can continue stubbornly toward denial. Once in denial, I will probably require some form of confrontation (either internal or external) to move upward toward self-awareness.

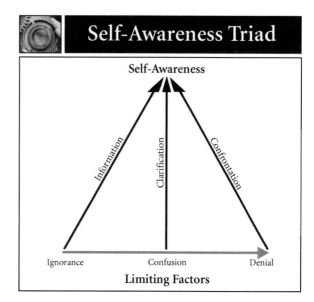

Cultivating self-awareness is a crucial step in the journey toward personal growth. No form of assessment will be effective until you are willing to confront facts and embrace truth. An important benchmark in personal maturity, especially for leaders, is the choice to separate our sense of self-worth from the way others respond to our ideas, decisions, and behaviors. In making this choice, we give permission to others to reject our ideas, question our decisions, or critique our behavior without rejecting us as individuals. This choice is the essence of self-awareness. It opens an expansive gateway to growth, empowering others to offer constructive criticism.

Choosing Self-Awareness

How I respond to new information is always my decision to make. I can choose to take the information constructively, or I can allow it to rally my insecurities, driving me into denial and widening my awareness gap even further. Even if the motives of those who criticize me are impure, I can usually benefit from their input. By refusing to take their comments personally, I can mine whatever nugget of truth is buried under the trash. This process is not easy, and the underlying decision to separate identity from performance must be reinforced constantly, but the results of choosing self-awareness are well worth the effort.

In the World War II action movie *U-571*, Matthew McConaughey plays the role of Andy Tyler, a submarine lieutenant who is denied an opportunity to command his own sub. Tyler soon learns the reason his dream was dashed; his commanding officer, Captain Dahlgren, actually discouraged the navy from promoting the young lieutenant.

In a powerful exchange of words, Tyler challenges his CO's decision, arguing that he has more than paid his dues and is ready to lay his life on the line for his crew. Captain Dahlgren, played by Bill Paxton, responds by saying: "I'm not questioning *your* bravery. Are you willing to lay *their* lives on the line?" The question leaves Tyler stunned. Before he has a chance to respond, the senior officer continues:

> You see, you hesitate. As a captain, you can't. You have to act. If you don't, you put the entire crew at risk. Now that's the job. It's not a science. You have to be able to make hard decisions based on imperfect information, asking men to carry out orders that may result in their deaths. And if you're wrong, you suffer the consequences. If you are not prepared to make those decisions, without pause, without reflection, then you've got no business being a submarine captain.

At that moment, Andy Tyler's awareness gap was exposed. He was given the information that showed precisely where he needed to grow in order to realize his dream. The remainder of the film compellingly illustrates Andy's journey from ignorance through confusion and denial to complete self-awareness.

Without self-awareness, you cannot analyze your D/A Differential because you don't know what you don't know. Without that information—and, more important, a willingness to accept it—you cannot construct a meaningful growth plan that will focus your mental energy on the most strategic elements of your capacity challenge. Unlike Lieutenant Tyler, most of us do not pursue our dreams in a life setting where the stakes are so high that people have to tell us the truth and we have to listen. That's why we need to choose self-awareness by cultivating a network of meaningful relationships and empowering those around us to expose the gaps in our self-knowledge.

Gaining Outside Assessment

If you are serious about cultivating self-awareness, you will recognize the need for 360-degree feedback on your capacity. You will identify a few trusted members of your inner circle to help you see through the blind spots and close your awareness gap. The key word here is *trusted*. You need more than a cadre of yes-men to cut through self-awareness fog. Use wisdom and good judgment when making your list. Solicit input from people to whom you relate in several life domains: personal, family, vocation, Kingdom, and community.

You will want to refine your own set of feedback questions, but you can start with a few that I find helpful:

- What aspect of my capacity should I be developing now in order to position me to realize my life dreams?

- Have you observed any blind spots in my life that keep me from seeing areas in which I need to grow? If so, what do I need to know in order to close this awareness gap?

- What personal growth goals do you think I should focus on if I am to play to my strengths?

- What character weaknesses should I address to ensure a strong foundation for my personal legacy?

- Do you see anything that suggests my life is out of balance or in need of renewed focus?

- Is there anything else you can share that will help me identify goals for my upcoming growth cycle?

When you ask people for feedback, remind them of your commitment to separate your identity from your ideas, decisions, and actions. Assure them that you will not interpret their responses as a personal attack and that you truly want to inventory your entire life, including the aspects that others may see while you do not.

SYSTEMATIC SELF-ASSESSMENT

During my earliest forays into personal growth planning, I resisted using a formal self-assessment tool. I was afraid the process would become too mechanical or impersonal. But as I began to coach others, it became clear that asking someone to perform a self-assessment armed only with a blank piece of paper was not very productive. That pushed me to identify a set of assessment categories that could serve as prompts or tools for increasing self-awareness. The five categories I developed are:

- *Spirituality*   Dealing with issues of character, faith, and moral-centeredness

- *Identity*   Dealing with the six components of the Identity Profile (personality, passion, talents, skills, spiritual gifts and dreams)

- *Responsibility* Dealing with the life domains (personal, family, vocation, Kingdom, and community)

- *Destiny*   Dealing with life mission

- *Legacy*   Dealing with finishing well and ultimate contributions[2]

Using only the five categories to perform a self-assessment yielded results that were marginally better than the blank-piece-of-paper approach, so I developed a more detailed Self-Assessment Tool. Here is a description of each assessment category. If you are to arrive at complete self-awareness, you must examine your life in each of these areas. (The entire Self-Assessment Tool is available free at www.KeepGrowingInc.com.)

Spirituality

Nearly all people recognize that they are spiritual beings. But how do you measure spirituality? Is there an objective marker of spiritual capacity? I believe that a vibrant and growing relationship with God is the foundation for effectiveness in all of life. More than talents, gifts, or training, the powerful presence of God in the life of a leader is the essential ingredient for realizing dreams and creating a lasting legacy.

This macro-leadership principle is reinforced by the example of Moses, who, after leading the Israelites out of Egypt, was offered the chance to enter the Promised Land with an angelic escort. But there was a condition: God wouldn't be there. When it came to a choice between realizing a dream and experiencing God's presence, Moses' decision was an easy one. He rejected the offer out of hand, saying, "If your Presence does not go with us, do not send us up from here."[3]

I believe that Moses was able to make this choice so quickly because he had experienced true intimacy with God. The biblical narrative that tells this part of Moses' story includes the interesting parenthetical comment that God spoke to Moses "face to face as a man speaks with his friend."[4] There is no dream, no goal, no worthy pursuit that could compare with knowing God and living in His presence. Having experienced this level of relationship with God, Moses was not about to trade it for the empty shell of personal success. Realizing your dream at the cost of your soul is always a bad bargain.

God-inspired dreams cannot be realized with human effort alone. If you shut God out of the process, all the dream chasing and growth planning in the world will leave you empty-handed, with only regret to show for all your striving. You must give attention in every growth cycle to the cultivation of a vibrant relationship with God.

Identity

Identity may be the most comprehensive category of personal assessment. You will find enough raw material in this category to generate a lifetime of personal growth. Most of your capacity issues will flow from the six components of your Identity Profile. Let's review them.

Personality. Self-aware people understand their personality and temperament. They have accepted who they are as God made them. Trying to morph from one temperament type to another is really an act of denial. In assessing this subcategory of your life, the goal is to discover and understand how you naturally relate to others, process information, and charge your physical or emotional batteries. To do so, you may find it helpful to use an additional tool, such as the Myers-Briggs Personality Type Indicator or the DiSC Personality Profile.[5]

Passions. The Listening and Processing stages of the Dream Cycle almost always stir inner passions of one kind or another. Passions are like interests on steroids. Self-aware people actively seek to bridle their passions and constructively channel these inner currents of desire. Your passions, when woven together, form a rope strong enough to support your dreams.

Amazingly, many people seem to have little awareness of their own passions. You will recognize the seeds of passion in the interests and causes that draw you to spend time learning, participating in activities, recruiting others to join you, or enduring hardships. However intuitive or mystical this element may seem, include it in your self-assessment. You must become aware of the inner passions that drive you to action.

Talents. I have already mentioned the idea that talents become strengths when combined with knowledge and skill. That makes it vitally important that you identify your talents. You cannot maximize these God-given abilities until you are aware of them. Self-aware people harness their innate abilities by taking conscious steps to develop them as strengths.[6]

Skills. A major aspect of building your capacity is increasing your competency in essential skills. The closer you get to the Planning stage of the Dream Cycle, the clearer the picture you will have of what skills you need in order to realize your dream. Unfortunately, many people see skill building as a personal development card trick that begins with "Pick a card, any card." It is not just *any* skill that you must develop. You must develop the specific skills that will leverage your strengths. And remember, any dream worth pursuing cannot be accomplished by you alone. You will need other people to help you, using their skills to complement your own. Don't give in to the temptation to develop skills outside of your identity, skills that should be brought to the dream by those with whom you share it.

Spiritual Gifts. God is your number one ally in personal development. He wants you to become and do everything for which you were created. In fact, every aspect of your Identity Profile is the result of His handiwork. That is especially true of spiritual gifts—abilities imparted to Christ's followers for the purpose of serving others.

You do not need to know what your spiritual gifts are in order to use them, but you can't develop them on purpose until you become aware of them. A number of tools for discovering your spiritual gifts are available. I recommend their use in combination with coaching from a mature leader to help you process this piece of your identity puzzle.[7]

Dreams. Yes, we're here again, knocking on the door of the most important component in your Identity Profile—an awareness of the dreams locked inside you. I have defined a dream as a compelling awareness of what could or should be, accompanied by a growing sense of responsibility to do something about it. Once you have a clear picture of your preferred future, you can cultivate the self-awareness needed to accurately measure your D/A Differential. That information is essential if you are to grow on purpose and realize your dream.

Responsibility

Although life is an integrated whole, you play various roles within it, each having a set of expectations and responsibilities. I've referred to these roles as *life domains*. The real world is never as neat and tidy as hoped for, and the boundaries between life domains are porous. Self-aware people understand the interconnection of their life domains and keep the bigger picture of their lives in view as they pursue their dreams. As with an organic system, a change in one life domain inevitably affects the others. It is not possible to construct a firewall between your life domains. As you conduct a systematic self-assessment, give attention to each of the following areas of responsibility.

Personal Life. No matter what your family status, you have an identity of your own and you are ultimately responsible for your own health, emotions, and general well-being. Self-aware people understand that the race toward a dream is more often a marathon than a sprint. Growth planning rightly includes the personal dimension.

Family Life. A paradox of high-intensity dreamers is that they often find themselves squeezed between what appear to be conflicting goals: realizing a dream and participating in family life. If your dream is God-inspired, however, loving your family and realizing your life goals will *never* be mutually exclusive. If pursuing your dream is harming your family, you either have the wrong dream or have taken the wrong path in pursuing it. Self-aware people consciously test the validity of their dreams against their responsibilities to their family.

Vocational Life. One of the largest investments people make—of both time and money—is in their careers. No wonder our culture has come to associate being with doing. Your life consists of much more than your work, but a great deal of your energy and thought power will be expended in this life domain. You cannot ignore your work when assessing yourself. If you are to be successful in pursuing your dream, you must be fully aware of how it is integrated with your vocation.

Kingdom Life. God-inspired dreams always add value to other people. Regardless of the social arena in which your dream is played out—business or education, government or church, entertainment or journalism—your dream should season the world with a taste of God that makes it hungry for more. For me, the Kingdom life domain is anchored in, but not limited to, a local church. As you take inventory of yourself, identify the ways in which your life advances God's purpose on earth.

Community Life. Ironically, many of us readily affirm the need to have an active Kingdom life but blatantly ignore the needs of people in our communities. Like commuters passing the scene of an accident, we often opt for rubbernecking or complaining rather than making a serious effort to fix the problems in our world. Sadly, those who score highest in an assessment of spirituality often score the lowest in responsibility for community. Truly self-aware people understand that volunteerism and community service go beyond church pews to soup kitchens and AIDS clinics. As you assess your areas of responsibility, examine the ways in which you contribute to the well-being of those around you.

Destiny

Your destiny is the sovereign purpose for which you have been created. Destiny fulfillment is the ultimate win/win. When you fulfill your destiny, God receives great glory, you receive great joy, and His purposes are strategically advanced. Your dreams are to your destiny what stars are to a solar system. Some stars shine brighter than others, but they all shed light, and each one marks the way toward your life's great mission.

Your awareness of your destiny will grow over time. Eventually, you will arrive at a clear enough awareness of your destiny that you can express it in a personal mission statement. Many people find it necessary to enlist the help of a mentor or coach in clarifying their life's mission and constructing a personal mission statement. Once you have crafted that statement, it will become a filter for your dreams, quickly straining out those that do not advance your purpose.

My life purpose is to inspire and equip the people around me (especially leaders) to grow on purpose, discover their destiny, and join with God in blessing the nations. My primary reason for writing this book is to create a resource that will advance that purpose—a resource that can travel where I cannot. Awareness of my destiny has helped me make progress in realizing my dreams. Assessing your own destiny will lend the same power to you.[8]

Legacy

Your legacy can be a difficult component of your life to assess because it involves the future. To assess your legacy, you must evaluate the factors or trends that point toward the contribution that you will ultimately make. Three priority questions shed light on the legacy category:

- How will I finish?

- What will I leave behind?

- How will I be remembered?

How you finish added to what you have accomplished will determine how you are remembered. As an expectant mother is connected to her child by an umbilical cord, so you are connected to your legacy by the cord of destiny. That cord is cut not when you are born—but when you die.

Saint Paul was obsessed with finishing well and leaving a legacy of faithfulness for others to follow. Paul capsulized that desire in a letter to some of his followers. He wrote:

> You've all been to the stadium and seen the athletes race. Everyone runs; one wins. Run to win. All good athletes train hard. They do it to get a gold medal that tarnishes and fades. You're after one that's gold eternally. I don't know about you, but I'm running hard for the finish line. I'm giving it everything I've got. No sloppy living for me! I'm staying alert and in top condition. I'm not going to get caught napping, telling everyone else about it and then missing out myself.[9]

Neither am I.

Self-aware people envision the end at the beginning and take proactive steps to shape their legacy. Are you fully aware of the legacy that you are leaving?

SELF-ASSESSMENT GUIDELINES

You should aim to take inventory once a year, just as a retail store does. The best time to conduct your self-assessment is at the close of your growth cycle. This will become one means of measuring your progress toward your growth goals. (You can use the Self-Assessment Tool available free at wwwKeepGrowingInc.com to more thoroughly evaluate each of the assessment categories described above.) As you conduct your self-assessment, keep these principles in mind.

The Age Correlation

First, there is a relationship between your age and the relative importance of each assessment category. Each of the five assessment categories will command varying levels of priority at different stages of life. Although the need to assess spirituality is consistent for people of every age, the priority of the others may change from one life stage to the next. Identity, for example, is a high priority for people in their twenties. Later in life, most aspects of the identity category are less important. Once a person becomes aware of his or her temperament and how it affects others, there is little need to focus on it. Passions and dreams may be revisited occasionally, but a person's identity is not likely to undergo radical changes later in life. It's wise not to spend an inordinate amount of time re-scrutinizing identity in each growth cycle.

Destiny usually becomes a critical concern for people in their later twenties or thirties. Once determined, a person's life mission is not likely to be altered dramatically and probably will not need in-depth assessment. Only certain aspects of the responsibility category are relevant to people under age thirty; legacy becomes a critical concern at midlife. This is not to suggest that people of a given age have *no* need to assess each category of life, only that the priority for various categories generally corresponds to a person's age and stage of life. The chart below shows the general relationship between personal growth assessment categories and age.

Priority of Growth Categories by Age

Category	Under 20	20-30	30-40	40-50	50-60	60+
Spirituality	X	X	X	X	X	X
Identity*	X	X	X	X	X	X
Responsibility**	X	X	X	X	X	X
Destiny		X	X	X		
Legacy			X	X	X	X

* Once all the areas of the Identity Assessment have been thoroughly addressed, only the giftedness component (talents, skills, spiritual gifts) will continue to be emphasized.

** In most cases only the peronal, family, and Kingdom roles will be emphasized in the Responsibility Assessment for those under age twenty.

The Fear Factor

Second, you must avoid being overwhelmed by the results of a personal assessment. An honest self-assessment in each of the five categories will always generate more possible growth goals than can be included in one growth cycle. That can be intimidating, but don't worry about acting on all of those goals right now. Concentrate on taking inventory and looking for potential growth areas. In the next chapter, you'll learn how to develop a growth action plan, which includes prioritizing growth areas and selecting the ones that belong in the current cycle. For now, simply being aware of the need for growth is a step in the right direction. The increased self-awareness that comes with a thorough assessment will heighten your sense of humility and position you for future growth.

The Negativity Trap

Third, when doing your personal growth assessment, be honest with yourself but not overly critical. After spending some time on self-examination, you may begin to think, *Wow . . I've really blown it! I'll never be able to grow in every area of my life.* Be alert to the propensity we all have for negative self-talk; it only interrupts the growth process. Actively resist these lies. Take a balanced view of your life by thinking of your capacity challenge as a growth trigger that will open the door to accelerated learning.

The Progress Marker

Finally, reflect on the positive attributes that you discover during your personal growth inventory. Recognize and celebrate the areas in which you are doing well in addition to noting the areas that need improvement. Give yourself a pat on the back as you recognize growth. Thank God for being your number-one growth ally. Keep journal notes of the ways you are progressing toward your dreams.

A WORD OF ENCOURAGEMENT

In order to grow, you must know where you need to grow. In order to see that need, you must do two things: (1) cultivate self-awareness and (2) conduct a systematic personal assessment using an instrument such as the Personal Growth Assessment Tool. Beware of trivializing this process by skimming lightly over the assessment, assuming that you are ready for the next step. Regardless of how mature you may already be, consistent, thorough self-examination continues to be one key that unlocks the door to your dreams.

I realize that this kind of self-discovery may seem excessive to you. It may push the outer limits of your personal growth galaxy. But consider what's at stake. Right now you could be staring at a paradigm shift that if rejected will leave you trapped far below the point where your dream intersects your potential. Don't turn back now. Remember, your dreams are at stake. Pretending is no substitute for growing. You can do this!

LEVERAGE POINTS

1. Review the Capacity Index you created in response to chapter 1. How might increased self-awareness affect the size of your P/A or D/A Differential? What steps can you take to increase your self-awareness?

2. Make a list of trusted friends who could help you conduct an outside assessment. Review the list of questions for outside assessment on page 108. What questions would you add to this list?

3. Review the five categories of assessment on page 109. Which of these have you been most apt to overlook in your personal growth planning? How may that have affected your development so far?

4. Do a personal growth assessment using the free Self-Assessment Tool from www.KeepGrowingInc.com or one of your own making. Develop a list of possible personal growth goals in preparation for the next step, creating a plan of action.

NINE

A Bridge to Your Dreams

Developing
a Plan of Action

On one occasion during the Civil War, General Stonewall Jackson was marching his troops through Virginia when they came to a river that could not be forded. They needed to construct a bridge. Jackson ordered the troops to set up camp for the night and instructed his engineers to immediately begin planning how to get the army across the river. After dismissing the engineers, Jackson met with the wagon master, instructing him to move the wagon train to the other side of the river as soon as possible.

The wagon master worked through the night, gathering rocks, fence posts, logs, and other available materials to construct a functional bridge. At dawn the next day, the wagon master reported to General Jackson that the wagons and troops were all across the river, awaiting his instructions. When Jackson asked about the engineers, the wagon master said, "They are in their tent drawing pictures of a bridge."

Assessment is an important step in growing to reach your dreams, but assessment alone is not enough. It must be closely followed by action. Assessment without action is like a picture of a bridge—it shows what is needed but does nothing, by itself, to advance the solution. If you are to realize your dreams, you must build a bridge from where you are to the preferred future that you envision.

Moving from assessment to action requires a subtle shift in outlook. The assessment process focuses on the question, In what areas do I need to grow? The creation of an action plan focuses on the question, What practical steps can I take to cultivate growth? The answer to that question comprises five important steps. Let's consider each one.

STEP ONE: CULTIVATE GROWTH ATTITUDES

The first step in action planning is to cultivate the attitudes that lead to growth. The keyword for this step is *responsibility*.

This step may not seem like part of action planning, but taking command of your thoughts is anything but passive. It would be hard to overstate the impact of your attitude on the personal growth process. Leadership author and speaker John Maxwell says, "Your attitude—not intelligence, talent, education, technical ability, opportunity, or even hard work—is the main factor that determines whether you will live your dream."[1] No one can make you grow. You must choose to grow, and accepting responsibility for your continued growth hinges on your attitude.

As a young leader, Winston Churchill understood the connection between attitude and personal growth. Serving as a correspondent for a British newspaper during the Boer War, young Churchill wanted to get as close to the action as possible. He traveled with a group of soldiers on an armored train to the front lines. En route, the train was ambushed. Once Churchill realized the seriousness of the situation, he offered his services to the commanding officer. Churchill's actions were heroic. One of the soldiers later wrote, "His presence and way of going on were as much good as fifty men would have been."

After helping to rescue twenty men under heavy fire from Boer soldiers, Churchill was taken captive. As a prisoner, he argued for his release based on the fact that he was a war correspondent and not a uniformed soldier. But his heroic actions in the heat of battle had nullified his protection as a journalist. He pleaded his case in letters to his family and the Prince of Wales, hoping they would be able to secure his release, but they were powerless to help. He spent his twenty-fifth birthday as a prisoner in South Africa.

Rather than wallowing in self-pity, Churchill decided to make the best of his situation. He took charge of his attitude and resolved to find some way to use this experience for his future good. He convinced his captors to allow him to become a member of the Transvaal State Library, where he used his time to read and study. In a letter to the Prince of Wales, he wrote, "Although it is irritating to be out of everything while so much is doing, I have a secure refuge, and I shall hope, philosophically, to improve my education." Within a matter of days, he escaped by climbing over the wall and embarking on a harrowing three-hundred-mile trip to the border of Transvaal. Years later, while serving as Britain's home secretary with oversight of the prison system, Churchill ensured that prisoners would have access to a library. He believed that those who wanted to learn and grow should have every opportunity.[2]

Another significant element of a growth attitude is humility. Humility is to growth what headwaters are to a river. From this single, often hard-to-find source, a mighty river is formed that winds its way toward a wide-open sea of possibilities. Humility empowers us to say "I don't know," "I was wrong," or "I need help." In each case, humility opens the floodgate of learning, and there is nothing passive about it.

If you question this point, think about the antithesis of humility: pride. Nothing stifles personal growth faster than pride. The fruits of pride are stubbornness, closed-mindedness, and hypocrisy, just to name a few. Pride places an artificial boundary on learning. A prideful attitude is like a bouncer at the doorway of your brain, checking the credentials of every source of knowledge. Legions of intellectual benefits are turned away because they are not "on the list."

Have you ever been too prideful to learn? Take a brief mental inventory. When was the last time you learned from a child? Have you ever learned from your subordinates? How do you respond when people with less experience than you teach a seminar or lead a meeting? Too often these and other learning opportunities do not make it past the bouncer—we reject them because they are not on our personal growth guest list. In the normal course of life, we all encounter a variety of learning opportunities that we will miss out on if we lack humility.

In a chemical laboratory, two elements may be mixed together with no resulting change. A catalyst is needed to trigger a reaction. Humility is a catalyst for learning because it produces teachability. It is impossible to learn without being teachable.

I've already stated that God is your number one ally when it comes to personal growth. But I must point out that there is a condition to that promise: it hinges on your attitude. "God opposes the proud but gives grace to the humble."[3] To willfully place yourself at odds with your Creator makes you more than proud; it makes you foolish.

STEP TWO: PRIORITIZE GROWTH AREAS

The second step in creating a personal growth action plan is to prioritize the areas in which you need growth. The keyword for this step is *selectivity*.

If you have adopted a humble, teachable attitude, you're ready to revisit the potential growth areas that you identified during your personal growth assessment. These growth possibilities are like a list of targets from which you will choose in order to ensure strategic progress in your personal growth. After completing a thorough assessment, most of us will be in what a military analyst might call a target-rich environment. The challenge is not finding something to shoot at but selecting the targets that will produce the greatest return for your effort.

Another way to think of this process is as selecting the route for a journey. You are on a journey from your actual capacity toward the realization of your dreams. There is always more than one way to get from one place to another. A wise traveler selects the route carefully to avoid delays and makes the most efficient use of resources. Prioritizing your growth needs is selecting the best pathway for your growth journey. The process is highly subjective, but these steps will help you begin to place your growth areas in order of importance.

List All Possible Growth Areas

Begin by reviewing the results of your outside assessment. Group the feedback you received from trusted members of your inner circle into the appropriate assessment categories: Spirituality, Identity, Responsibility, Destiny, and Legacy. Look for common threads in the feedback, and make note of suggested areas that show up more than once, especially if they come from different sources.

Next, review the information from the self-assessment you performed using the Personal Growth Assessment Tool. Once you have merged the results from the two sources of information, highlight possible growth goals in each category.

Narrow the List

Later in this chapter, you'll learn how to determine the number of goals you should have on your active list. As a first step in narrowing your list to a manageable number, consider the following questions.

Which Growth Areas Promise the Most Strategic Return? All personal growth is an investment in your future, but not all goals produce the same rate of return. The most strategic growth areas are those that address your capacity challenge directly and have the greatest potential for reducing your D/A Differential. Increased self-awareness, the ability to state your life mission, and improved time management are likely to be high-return areas of growth, especially early in the growth process, because each of them is a prerequisite for future growth.

Confusion about the selection of strategic growth areas occurs most often in Phase 1 of the Dream Cycle. The transition from Dreaming to Planning—from Phase 1 to Phase 2—will naturally generate increased clarity in selecting strategic goals. If you are in Phase 1, focus your attention on the Spirituality and Identity categories.

Which Growth Areas Relate to My Present Life Stage? As emphasized in the previous chapter, there is a relationship between a learner's age and the priority of various assessment categories. A strategic growth goal for a mid-career leader, such as refining a mission statement or identifying one's legacy, will be extremely difficult for a younger, emerging leader to complete. And life-stage dreams often call for different skill sets than life dreams. Just as the sources of motivation for growth will change over a lifetime, so will the priority given to various growth areas. Choose growth goals that relate most directly to your current stage of life.

Which Growth Areas Will Enable Me to Achieve Greater Balance? Remember the importance of having a holistic growth plan. A balanced plan need not always have one goal from each assessment category, but balance is achieved by discerning which life domains are in need of special attention in a given growth cycle.

On Which Areas Is God Leading Me to Focus? Prioritizing and selecting personal growth goals is not a purely cognitive, analytical process. The Timing component of the Dream Cycle often swings on the hinges of God's intervention. Selecting the right growth goals cannot be done with a spreadsheet in which the data is simply placed into the correct fields and processed when you hit "enter." These choices must be made with discernment and wisdom that goes beyond the scope of purely rational thinking.

Perform a Growth-Goal Audit

By now you have identified a preliminary list of priority goals for your action plan. But how many goals should you choose? There is no simple answer to that important question. You must customize your growth plan to fit you. The best way to narrow down the possibilities for yourself is to perform a growth-goal audit, giving attention to two specific areas: time and finances.

Time. Not every growth goal will require the same amount of time and energy to complete. The real question is not how many growth goals to include but how much time is available to pursue them. Performing a growth-goal time audit begins with the question, How much time can I devote to personal growth activities *per week*?

There will be weeks in which you have no time at all for growth activities because of unplanned emergencies or scheduled responsibilities that require intense bursts of activity. Just estimate a reasonable weekly average. You will need to revisit and fine-tune your time budget after creating the specific growth activities of your plan. The more experienced you are in the growth-planning process, the easier it will be to look at your list of prospective goals and make initial determinations about the amount of time they will require.

Finances. Personal growth will cost you more than time. A financial audit asks, How much money can I invest in personal growth activities during *this growth cycle*? As you complete your action plan, you will inevitably find yourself buying books, magazines, and CDs, attending seminars, and perhaps enrolling in formal training. If you set a goal to read twenty-four books next year but only purchased five books last year, you will need to make some room in your budget to accommodate your goal. Keep in mind that these expenses may be the best investment you can make, well worth the sacrifice they might require in other areas. During your initial planning time, you may not have accurate cost information on each proposed activity. Once you have researched the cost of your selected goals, you will want to revisit your financial audit. Beware of moving forward with your action plan without counting the cost. If you do, you will be tempted to give up because you simply cannot afford to follow through with your goals.

Step Three: Envision Growth Attributes

The third step in creating a personal growth action plan is to envision the growth attributes that you hope to attain. The keyword for this step is *expectancy*.

Herb True said, "Many people succeed when others do not believe in them. But rarely does a person succeed when he does not believe in himself." An important part of creating an action plan is envisioning the results of growth in your life and assuming a posture of expectancy. When you visualize yourself embodying the results of your personal growth goals, you gain the believability and sense of expectation that undergirds the growth process.

Dr. Charles Garfield has extensively researched the idea of peak performance in both sports and business. While working with NASA, he was exposed to astronauts who envisioned every aspect of their mission in simulation exercises before going into space. Dr. Garfield's research also documented that world-class athletes and other peak performers repeatedly visualized their achievements as part of their preparation.[4] They saw themselves winning the race, achieving their goals and realizing their dreams.

Personal affirmation statements help you visualize the result of your growth goal by providing a word picture of the desired outcome. Writing affirmation statements is a necessary skill for growing toward your goal. These statements begin with the words *I am* followed by a verb and an outcome based descriptive statement. Here's an example. Several years ago I wrote this affirmation statement as part of my growth plan: "I am benefiting from the stimulating interaction and increased accountability that flows from vulnerable, authentic relationships with others."

One of the most important action steps associated with this goal was inviting several men to join me twice a month to share openly about issues we were facing and offer mutual encouragement, counsel, and prayer.

Initiating those meetings was an action step, but the result was what I'd envisioned in my affirmation statement. Remember, a good affirmation statement focuses on the *outcome*, not the *method* of achieving it. One way to test your affirmation statements is to ask, If other people were to evaluate my progress based on these statements, would they have enough specific information to provide meaningful feedback?

STEP FOUR: PURSUE GROWTH ASSETS

The fourth step in creating a personal growth plan is to pursue growth assets. The keyword for this step is *creativity*.

Now that you have a prioritized list of areas in which to grow and have envisioned the results you expect in each area, you must identify the assets at your disposal for achieving those results. A key to this part of the process is creativity. Many people become discouraged quickly after making a list of growth priorities because they don't know how to develop themselves in each area. There are always methods of growth available, although it may take some creative thought to identify them. You can find a way to make progress, even it takes you well outside of the box.

One of my favorite examples of this kind of informed ingenuity comes from the life of J. Hudson Taylor, who served as a historical role model in chapter 5. At age seventeen, Hudson had a powerful destiny experience when he sensed a divine call to go to China as a missionary. His life dream was born. Recognizing that it would be several years before he could go, Taylor chose to prepare as best he could. He had an intuitive awareness of his D/A Differential, and he knew where to grow if he were to realize his God-inspired dream.

Taylor reasoned that life in China would be much more demanding than what he had experienced in Britain, so he got rid of his cozy feather bed in preparation for what was sure to be a more rugged existence. He knew also that he would need to learn Mandarin in order to communicate with the Chinese, a challenging growth goal since there were no resources available—no Berlitz courses, no instructors, no videos, no computer-based translation tools. Most people would have given up on learning Mandarin in advance of actually going to China, but not Hudson Taylor. He learned the meaning of five hundred Chinese characters in a matter of weeks without the aid of a teacher, grammar book, or dictionary. How? By comparing a Chinese version of the Gospel of Luke with an English Bible. Here is how Taylor described his methods to his sister Amelia:

> We find a short verse in the English version, and then look out a dozen or more (also in English) that have one word in common with it. We then turn up the first verse in Chinese, and search through all the others for some character in common that seems to stand for the English word. This we write down on a slip of paper as its probable equivalent. Then we look all through the Chinese Gospel for this same character in different connections. It occurs as a rule pretty frequently. And if in every case we find the same word in the English version, we copy the character in ink into our dictionary, adding the meaning in pencil. Afterwards, if further acquaintance shows it to be the true meaning, we ink that over also. At first we made slow progress, but now we can work much faster, as with few exceptions we know all the most common characters.[5]

Hudson Taylor's example demonstrates the way assets can be brought to bear on a specific growth need if creativity is combined with motivation. As you look for assets to use in implementing your growth action plan, start your search in these categories.

Learning from Experience

Learning from experience is to your growth plan what practice is to an athlete. Look over your list of growth categories and expected results and ask, How could I begin to gain experience in this area? What could I start doing that would provide me with a real-life laboratory? How could I practice this skill in order to gain confidence as well as ability? Once you get some initial experience, reflect on that experience to identify ways of improving in the future.

If you have a goal of becoming a better speaker, find safe and appropriate places to give a talk. If you want to become a better writer, start writing consistently. If you want to learn another language, get around people who speak that language. Give yourself opportunities to gain experience in areas that relate to your growth goals, and then be disciplined in evaluating both how you did and what you learned from it.

All this is really common sense, but let me remind you of the role of humility in the learning process. Standing at the bottom of your personal growth curve and staring up at the steep incline that leads to where you want to be is a humbling experience. No one likes to look foolish or risk being embarrassed. We all have expended bits of mental energy replaying memories of negative experiences; they automatically flood our minds when we think about learning in a real-life laboratory. In order to grow, you will have to decide that keeping pace on the journey to your dream is more important than saving face.

My grandfather used to say that experience is the best teacher, but if you can learn in any other way, do it. I would modify my grandfather's proverb by saying experience *can* be the best teacher. We have all met people who do the same foolish things over and over again. Experience is of value only if we choose to learn from it. My grandfather's point was that we should learn from vicarious experience in addition to personal experience.

Personal experience can come only from your own journey; vicarious experience makes profitable use of the journeys of others. Vicarious learning is an important growth asset for two reasons. First, you don't have time to make all the mistakes you need to make to learn all that you need to learn. Second, the cost of some failure experiences is simply too high for you to learn from them and stay on course. That's why you need to learn from the journeys of others, especially great leaders who have gone before you. This form of vicarious learning is called historical mentoring. I have found it to be one of the most inspiring methods of personal growth. Almost every personal growth goal on your list could be connected to a vicarious learning experience through the focused study of a leader from the past.[6]

Learning from People

One of the most valuable assets in your personal growth toolbox is the network of people with whom you have developed or could develop a learning relationship. Remember the keyword associated with the first step in this plan: responsibility. You must accept responsibility for your personal growth. That means you cannot sit back and wait for your ideal mentor to come riding in on a white horse and create a customized learning environment for you. You need to look for people who can come alongside you and contribute to your personal growth. Here are a few hints for finding personal mentors or learning coaches.

Be Specific. When you enlist the help of others in your learning plan, define your growth goal specifically and state why you believe they could help you pursue it. Simply asking someone to be a mentor is a vague and somewhat intimidating proposal. Cut through the ambiguity and uncertainty by explaining why you believe having a mentor in the specific area is a high value. Affirm what you see in the prospective mentor that has drawn you to him or her. The conversation might go something like this. "I'm working on a personal growth plan for this year and one of my goals is to become a more effective communicator. I really admire your skill in that area. I imagine that you have worked hard at refining your natural gift in order to be so effective. I'd like to ask you to mentor me in that area, to help me grow as a communicator."

Set Reasonable Expectations. Emphasize your respect for your prospective mentor's time, and define your expectations for the relationship. An unstated expectation that sometimes accompanies mentoring is a social relationship, which can be time-intensive. There is nothing wrong with mentors developing a deeper relationship with mentees, but don't allow this often-unspoken expectation to create a barrier from the start. Acknowledge your awareness of your prospective mentor's busy schedule, and explain that you are asking for only a small amount of time, which will naturally be limited by two factors: your defined growth goal and the mentor's stated level of availability. If a deeper friendship develops, let it be initiated by the mentor and not imposed by the expectations that you bring to the relationship.

Commit to Follow Through. When approaching a prospective mentor, affirm your commitment to follow through on projects or assignments that may be given to you. Some mentors are understandably skeptical about requests for assistance because they have previously attempted to coach learners who had insufficient commitment or ulterior motives. Going public with your intention to apply yourself to this learning experience will both encourage your mentor and deepen your own resolve to maximize the opportunity.

Offer Compensation. It may be reasonable to compensate your mentor for his or her time. If so, offer to do so at the outset. If you are approaching a high-level leader who is routinely asked to mentor others, it may be necessary to demonstrate your high level of motivation. One-on-one time with such a leader may prove to be more valuable than a whole day at a conference. If you would be willing to pay for a conference, why not pay for customized interaction with a high-level leader? Ask yourself, How much do

I want this person to be part of my personal growth process? If you believe this mentor's involvement could be a crucial component in your growth plan, raise the stakes in some creative way by offering compensation.

The discipline of personal coaching is coming into its own, and there are many opportunities for one-on-one interaction with proven leaders that were not available ten years ago. Consider seeking out a personal growth coach to help you with the aspects of your growth plan that go beyond your available growth assets.[7]

Learning from Resources

Researchers estimate that we have generated more information in the last three decades than in the previous five thousand years. Over one thousand books are published every day. One weekday edition of the *New York Times* includes more information than the average person encountered in his or her entire lifetime in seventeenth-century England. If you need a book, magazine, or other resource related to a specific personal growth goal, it probably exists. Today one keyword search on an Internet search engine generates more results than I used to get in a half day of searching the library. If you find yourself at a loss to identify a set of resources (things like books, CDs, and, seminars) that can become growth assets in a specific area, turn to people in your network for help. Even if someone you've approached cannot serve as your mentor, he or she may be able to help direct you to the right resources to help you grow.

STEP FIVE: PARTICIPATE IN GROWTH ACTIVITIES

The final step in your personal growth plan is to participate in growth activities. The keyword in this area is *consistency.*

Former United States senator and professional basketball player Bill Bradley once shared advice he received from his father about the need to apply himself as an athlete. "When you are not practicing, someone else is. And when you meet him, he will beat you." If you want to realize your dreams, you will need to consistently participate in the activities outlined in your personal growth plan.

My wife, Sherry, is a great example of the value of consistency. We have been married since 1984, and we have four children. Sherry still weighs the same as she did when we got married, and the size four pants I got her for Christmas last year fit just fine. I often hear people say how much they wish they had her genetic predisposition for being thin, as if to suggest that she is in such great shape because of the luck of the DNA draw. I know that genetics do play a role in shaping one's physique, but I know also that Sherry does an aerobic workout three or four times each week. Her consistency in these health and fitness activities combined with discipline at the table have paid dividends over time. Thousands of people make plans each year to get in better shape. Some of them join health clubs, and others purchase state-of-the-art equipment for use at home. They have the best of intentions—as you probably do for your personal growth plan—but without consistent activity over time, they do not see results.

I once asked a friend if he was using the high-tech treadmill he bought and he said, "Sure, we use it all the time. It's the perfect place to hang the clothes we're going to wear the next day. It saves a lot of time in the morning."

I wish there were a surefire way to help people consistently turn good intentions into action. That would open the floodgates of personal growth because almost everyone has a desire to improve. While there is no simple answer to the consistency question, I have found four practical steps that help maintain the consistent practice of growth activities.

Post Your Goals

First, post your written growth plan in a visible location. In the next chapter, you'll learn how to use a Personal Growth Summary Sheet that integrates each component of your plan into a simple written document. I keep these summary sheets in a folder on my desk, and I often carry them with me on trips so I can review my progress. I transfer electronic versions of them to my PDA so I can review them when I arrive a few minutes early for a meeting. I also print a list of my affirmation statements and post them on a bulletin board near my desk. I want as many reminders of my plan as I can get. If I fall short on a goal, I know it will not be because I have forgotten it.

Review Affirmation Statements Regularly

Next, regularly review your personal growth affirmation statements. For many people, an exercise of this nature seems tacky, like slick mental gymnastics that belong on a late-night infomercial for a get-rich-quick scheme. But I assure you that if you write good affirmation statements for each of your personal growth goals and review them regularly, you will create momentum for action. You do not need to stand in front of a mirror every day repeating your written statements. Just find ways to reinforce your commitment to become what you are not yet. Affirm these verbal pictures of the results of working your plan. Go ahead. Swallow your pride, and do it out loud. At the very least, keep your affirmation statements posted near your desk or in some other visible place where you can refer to them often. This discipline will reinforce your sense of expectancy about who you will become as a result of working your plan.

Schedule Growth Activities

Third, schedule time for growth activities on your calendar. The growth goals outlined in any given cycle will take time from something else you are already doing—even if it is watching television or reading the paper. There is always competition for your personal growth time. Redirect your time allotment to create the space you need to pursue growth goals. The most efficient way to do that is by making a personal growth appointment with yourself, blocking that off on your calendar and guarding it carefully. I routinely say no to requests for my time that conflict with personal growth appointments I have made with myself. When asked to schedule that time elsewhere, I simply say, "I'm sorry. I can't meet then. I'm already booked for that time slot." Ultimately, making time for growth is a matter of priorities, and putting growth appointments on the calendar helps reinforce the decision to follow through.

Enlist Support

Finally, enlist the support of others who are willing to help you follow through. People who believe in and want you to realize your dreams can form a powerful personal growth safety net. Once you have established your goals, share them with those in your inner circle and ask them to keep you accountable for reaching them. The people who care most about you will give you the support you need to consistently act on your plan. Accountability relationships are so valuable in the personal growth process that I have devoted the entire next chapter to the subject.

WILL YOU DO IT?

Creating an action plan for personal growth involves cultivating growth attitudes, prioritizing growth areas, envisioning growth attributes, pursuing growth assets, and participating in growth activities. You have thoroughly assessed all aspects of your personal life, and that's good. You now have a picture of the bridge that will carry you to your dreams. The question is, will you cross it? Will you take action to grow into the person you need to be in order to realize your dreams?

LEVERAGE POINTS

1. Has your attitude toward personal growth been an asset or liability? Think of the last time you said "I don't know." How long ago was it? What does this say, if anything, about the presence of humility in your life?

2. Review your list of possible growth goals based on your personal assessment. Giving consideration to the principles outlined in this chapter, identify the goals you believe will be most strategic for this growth cycle.

3. Perform an initial time and finance audit of your list. Which activities will consume the most resources? Does that change their priority for this cycle?

4. Create affirmation statements for each of your possible goals, using the basic template: I am + verb (becoming, developing, etc.) + outcome-based descriptive statement of the results.

5. Make an initial list of the growth assets you might assemble for each of your affirmation statements; include people, resources, and experiences.

TEN

A Cord of Three Strands

Forming Accountability Partnerships

A ccountability. What comes to your mind when you hear that word? Are your first thoughts positive, negative, or neutral? Do you think of accountability as something like a speed bump that you prefer to avoid, or a guardrail that makes you feel safe?

Many people have a negative feeling about accountability. One of the underpinnings of American culture is rugged individualism. That pioneering spirit helped fuel the entrepreneurial explosion that has made the United States a global superpower and bastion of capitalism. But rugged individualism is a two-edged sword. An emphasis on individual rights tends to erode community, diminishing the caring scrutiny of others who have been empowered to speak truth into our lives. Only one out of every seven adults is currently in any type of serious accountability partnership. Perhaps more unfortunate, even fewer are eager to enter into such a relationship.[1]

Given the way most of us tend to avoid accountability, it is no wonder corporate America is in such a mess. Success—defined as profitability—has become a commercial sacrament that absolves leaders of the unethical means used to obtain it. We have cultivated a taste for loopholes, and we make liberal use of them in both our professional and private lives. Our avoidance of organizational accountability reflects a similar preference at the individual level.

Sources of accountability that could keep us on track and prod us toward realizing our dreams are often viewed as roadblocks to success.

Yet accountability is a valuable asset for growth. Although accountability provides no shortcut, it does provide a safety harness, and I cannot imagine trying to climb any of life's mountains without it. In fact, accountability plays such an important role in reaching your God-inspired dreams that I believe you would make progress in the Growing stage of your Dream Cycle even if you did nothing else but enter into a meaningful and consistent accountability relationship. And when you add to that relationship a specific personal growth plan, the results will be dramatic. You will grow fastest and best when you are in an intentional accountability relationship. That makes accountability an important key to realizing your dreams.

BASIC PRINCIPLES OF ACCOUNTABILITY

So far you've answered two important questions that feed your personal growth plan: In what areas should I pursue growth? And what practical steps can I take to cultivate growth? Now you'll consider a third: who can help me stay focused on growth? Before you answer that question, let's look at the big-picture issues of accountability.

Everyone Is Accountable

Everyone is accountable to someone for something at some time. Accountability is an inescapable part of everyday life. The police officer parked alongside the road is prepared to hold you accountable for driving within the speed limit. The Internal Revenue Service is going to hold you accountable for paying your taxes. If you are married, your spouse will probably ask if you took out the trash this week or did the laundry. If you are working on a graduate degree, your professor will have various methods for holding you accountable for learning. Your boss wants to know if you will meet the deadline on a current project.

And so it goes. Every one of us has multiple accountability relationships. The problem is that few people harness the power of accountability by selecting the right person for an accountability relationship and narrowing the focus of that relationship to important developmental issues. You are accountable. Will you use that accountability to help you grow?

We Accept Accountability for Success

We like to be held accountable for things we consistently do well. Remember the kid who always raised his hand in math class to remind the teacher when she forgot to collect the homework assignment? Why did he do that? He was looking for positive feedback, confident that he had done well. Unfortunately, he shredded my vain hope that I would get away without doing the assignment. I am sure you can relate. We all want someone to check up on us when we expect a reward for doing well. Using accountability in your growth plan will spur you to be your best.

We Resist Accountability for Failure

The flip side to reward is punishment, and we resist being held accountable for underachievement and character weaknesses. When we resist accountability, the root cause is usually some failure on our part to perform adequately. Think about how you feel heading into a staff meeting when you are caught up on your work compared to when you have missed important deadlines. The dread you feel when you're behind schedule does not stem from the staff meeting or from being held accountable; it stems from the failure to meet expectations.

It is fascinating to see how counterproductive our natural feelings are in this area. We regret our character weaknesses and underachievement; that is understandable. But then we resort to the childish game of "if you didn't see me do it, it never happened." We know better, of course, but we still have a hard time facing reality.

Accountability, however, does not bring pain. The pain comes from the underlying problem; accountability merely exposes it. Shedding more light on the work we have done may cause initial discomfort because it reveals hidden defects. But those defects cannot be corrected until they are seen. Since accountability not only exposes problems but also helps to minimize them, we should view it as a positive thing. One mark of maturity is a desire to improve coupled with an attitude that welcomes objective reality. Accountability is an aid to self-assessment, and you cannot grow without it.

Resistance Reveals Need

Generally, the areas of our lives in which we resist accountability are those in which our need for growth is the greatest. I don't need anyone to ask me whether I got enough calories this week; I enjoy eating and never need to be reminded to do it. But I will probably always benefit from someone confronting me about my need for regular exercise. My most challenging growth goals require not only my own personal discipline but also the help of a few committed friends in the form of accountability partnerships. It is likely that you have growth needs that you cannot address on your own. You may need accountability the most in the areas that you would most like to remain unseen.

THE BENEFITS OF ACCOUNTABILITY

King Solomon, perhaps the wisest man who ever lived, wrote about the value of accountability partnerships: "Two are better than one, because they have a good return for their work: If one falls down, his friend can help him up. But pity the man who falls and has no one to help him up! Also, if two lie down together, they will keep warm. But how can one keep warm alone? Though one may be overpowered, two can defend themselves. A cord of three strands is not quickly broken."[2]

Three helpful principles flow from this passage, and they point to the specific benefits of accountability partnerships.[3]

Accountability Increases Productivity

"Two are better than one, because they have a good return for their work." Accountability enhances productivity and effectiveness; it is like adding another set of hands on a project. There's a saying among leaders that goes like this: you don't get what you *expect*; you get what you *inspect*. The power of an accountability partnership comes from the permission that you grant for another person to inspect your growth progress and help you increase productivity.

Accountability Increases Resiliency

"If one falls down, his friend can help him up." One role of a good accountability partner is that of a cheerleader or encourager. When you feel like giving up after a bout of personal failure, your accountability partner can play a crucial role in motivating you to get going again. More is at stake than a single growth goal because your personal growth is an essential building block for realizing your dreams. At some point in your journey through the Dream Cycle, you will face a challenging moment that requires the encouragement, support, and accountability of those who are committed to helping you stay the course.

Accountability Increases Security

"Though one may be overpowered, two can defend themselves." Standing shoulder to shoulder with someone who is pulling for your success brings a deepened sense of security and confidence. It is easier to believe that you can throw off the many hindrances to your personal growth when you have the help of a trusted partner. Hearing words of encouragement and support from an accountability partner makes your own affirmation statements even more believable. Although you may have a natural tendency toward negative self-talk and dwelling on past failures, accountability relationships provide the strength and confidence to persevere.

TYPES OF ACCOUNTABILITY PARTNERSHIPS

Choosing the right accountability partner depends on understanding the type of accountability partnership that you intend. Different growth goals require different accountability formats and, therefore, different people to assist with them. I benefit greatly from my relationship with a general accountability partner with whom I connect each month to address spiritual issues, family priorities, and big-picture goals. But I make use of other accountability partnerships also, which fill specialized roles. Let's look briefly at the different kinds of accountability relationships before zeroing in on the selection of accountability partners.

Mentor

Mentor accountability is usually provided by a trusted advisor who is older, wiser, and more experienced than you are. When you are involved in a mentoring relationship, you give consent for the mentor to hold you accountable for the tasks and projects that flow from your interaction. Mentor accountability is helpful when you aim to acquire a specific skill. It is usually a top-down or one-sided relationship in which the mentor provides the accountability that helps you follow through on projects or assignments, but not vice versa.

Group

Group accountability is built upon the relationships and shared focus among three or more people. This format requires an equal level of trust between each member of the group. As the group size increases—especially beyond five or six—it is almost impossible to retain the level of trust, confidentiality, and vulnerability required to be effective. Focusing on different goals for each person can become awkward in a group setting. Group accountability is most effective when everyone in the group is pursuing a common growth goal.

Spouse

Your spouse can provide a powerful accountability partnership. In a healthy marriage, the vulnerability and honesty between a husband and wife reaches the deepest recesses of the heart. Who but your life partner would have a greater desire to serve as a catalyst for your growth? But spousal accountability can be fragile, especially when the marriage is under stress. Some marriage partners struggle to control the negative emotions that are brought to the surface by issues addressed in a partner's growth plan. There are times when accountability is best provided by someone other than a spouse.

One-to-One

One-to-one accountability is the highest and most flexible form of accountability partnerships other than that between husband and wife. Unlike mentor accountability, one-to-one accountability allows for a two-way relationship concerning both general life issues and specific growth goals. Since this type of partnership may deal with serious matters of the heart, it is advisable to engage in one-to-one accountability only with people of the same gender. That not only safeguards your personal integrity but also shields you against potential accusations of sexual harassment. One-to-one accountability is a powerful source of encouragement, and I include it as a primary component of my growth plan for every major goal.

Accountability Types

Accountability Type	Distinctive	Growth Plan Comments
Mentor	Top-down or one-sided in nature; unequal level of vulnerability	Useful when coaching is needed or no peer expertise is available
Group	Requires equal level of relationships among all group members; effective but fragile	Useful when there is a need for accountability on the same issue among all group members
Spouse	Effectiveness varies with the area of accountability; useful for very personal items	Can be difficult when marriage is under stress or with some sensitive areas
One-to-One	Highest level beyond spousal; allows two-way accountability for general and specific needs	Useful for almost every growth area; requires high level of trust and confidence

ENLISTING ACCOUNTABILITY PARTNERS

The basic rule for enlisting an accountability partner is to first select the right format, then identify the right person. On more than one occasion, I have been disappointed by the results of an accountability relationship because I chose the wrong partner. These guidelines will help you maximize the potential for success in accountability partnerships.

Match the Partner to the Need

The depth of your relationship with your accountability partner must be proportional to the sensitivity of the issue for which you wish to be held accountable. If you are working on a growth goal that relates to heart-level issues, you will need to find an accountability partner with whom you have a deep relationship. If you are seeking accountability for a relatively routine goal such as reading one book each month, nearly any friend or acquaintance could provide accountability. Match your need for sensitivity, confidentiality, and vulnerability with the depth of relationship you have with the potential partner.

Explain Your Aim

Don't expect prospective growth partners to fully grasp your intention without a thorough explanation. Most people have never been asked to serve in the role you have in mind. Don't take anything for granted. Tell your prospective accountability partner how this relationship fits into your personal growth plan and how you believe it will help you grow. Emphasize the fact that you are looking for someone to both encourage and confront you, someone who will lovingly challenge you with hard questions.

Some of your accountability partnerships will be one-way, meaning that your partner holds you accountable on certain points, but you do not hold him or her accountable for anything. Some people feel awkward pushing you to grow when they are not required to offer a similar level of vulnerability. Set them at ease from the start by framing the parameters of your relationship. Outline the boundaries for how frequently and in what manner you will communicate. Once per month is a good target for frequency of communication, and many effective accountability partnerships are carried out by e-mail.

Some of your growth goals will be projects you intend to accomplish in one day or during a specified period of time. In those cases, simply communicate the timetable to your accountability partner and ask him or her to check up on you a week before (to make sure you are still moving forward) and a week after (to see how you did).

Provide Specific Questions

Beyond encouraging and supportive words, the most important element of your accountability partnership will be the questions posed when you interact. Since these questions are so critical to the success of the relationship, you should assume the responsibility for crafting them. Provide your partner with a list of specific questions that you want to be asked. This will tell your accountability partner exactly what you need from him or her.

Suppose you have a goal to read twelve leadership books during your current growth cycle. You may want to give your accountability partner a set of questions like these for your monthly checkups.

- What is the title and author of the book you read this month?

- What is the most important leadership principle you learned from reading this book?

- Does anything you read need further clarification? If so, whom will you ask for help?

- Did you disagree with any substantive issue in the book? If so, what was it and why?

- In what ways are you applying the most practical idea or principle you learned?

- Would you recommend this book to other leaders? Why or why not?

Answering questions like these would add great value to the achievement of reading twelve books.

Request Prayer

Not all of my growth partners share my personal faith. I don't use that as a litmus test for accountability partnering. But many members of my relational network do share the conviction that God is my number one personal growth ally. If you are in a similar situation, be proactive about including this intangible value in accountability relationships by asking your partners to pray for your personal growth.

Perhaps you are in the opposite situation: you don't have a personal faith that is shared by many of your friends and associates. I challenge you to consider conducting this personal experiment. Ask some people of faith with whom you are acquainted to both hold you accountable and pray that God will bless your effort in a specific area of growth. Then see if you notice a difference in your progress toward that goal. What do you have to lose?

PRIORITIZING ACCOUNTABILITY NEEDS

You will certainly be pursuing more than one growth goal in any given cycle, and there may be more areas in which you need accountability than you have partners available. Four simple questions have helped me prioritize the areas in which I seek accountability and leverage the power of my relational network.

Which Goals Have the Highest Degree of Difficulty?

Just as you can look over your daily to-do list and intuitively discern which tasks will be the hardest to accomplish, you can weigh the difficulty of your growth goals. Arrange them in descending order, placing the ones that will stretch you the most at the top of the list. It is not hard to understand that the goals at the top will require the most intense support through accountability.

Which Goals Involve the Highest Level of Vulnerability?

Goals that require higher levels of transparency will move you to seek accountability near the inner circle of your relational network. As a result, you will always have a shorter list of potential accountability partners for these goals. Draw a circle next to each goal on your list: a small circle showing high vulnerability and the need for close accountability relationships, or a bigger circle showing low vulnerability with a wider selection of possible growth partners.

What Format Is Best Suited for Each Goal?

After considering the degree of difficulty and level of vulnerability associated with each growth goal, review the accountability formats to identify the best approach. The most common format—and usually the easiest to arrange—is one-to-one accountability. But don't neglect the others. In some cases, a mentor will be most effective. And including spousal and group accountability will widen your choice of accountability partners, increasing your overall accountability during the cycle.

Whom Should I Enlist for Each Goal?

This question brings you to the final step on this process—listing the names of prospective growth partners for each goal. For each of your top goals—those having a higher degree of difficulty—you may wish to ask two, three, or even four people to serve as growth partners. That creates *redundant accountability* so that even if one or two of your partners do not follow through, you will still be held accountable for those goals.

Once you have a good list of names for each goal, it is time to pull the accountability trigger by offering a specific invitation for these partners to join you in accountability relationships. It is wise to include with this invitation both the affirmation statement associated with your goal and the specific questions that you want your growth partners to ask. Also mention the frequency (how often you want to be in contact) and the format (e-mail, phone, in person) that you hope to maintain.

DREAM CYCLE ACCOUNTABILITY

No dream is realized in a single giant leap. All of your God-inspired dreams will be realized by making small steps behind the scenes, out of the limelight, twenty or thirty minutes at a time, day after day, in activities that may appear mundane, routine, and boring. Enlisting someone to tap you on the shoulder each month and ask "Have you realized your dream yet?" would be of no value. But regular contact from someone who shares your dream and will ask "Have you read a book since we last met?" "Did you exercise three times this week?" or "What have you done this month to practice public speaking?" will provide the power to stay on course in your Dream Cycle.

I have enlisted the help of many accountability partners over the years, and I have never once had someone respond negatively to my request for help. Not every growth partner follows through consistently, but there is very little chance that someone will be offended by your request. If enlisting an accountability partner were the only thing you did in order to advance your personal growth, I believe you would see noticeable improvement in the area that you selected. Add to that accountability a well-crafted personal growth plan, and the results will be explosive. Leverage the power of accountability, and you will realize your dreams.

LEVERAGE POINTS

1. What is your personal history with accountability? When was the last time you specifically engaged another person to hold you accountable for a developmental activity? How, if necessary, will you overcome your aversion to voluntary accountability?

2. Recall a personal growth goal that you did not reach. How might an accountability relationship have changed your results?

3. Review the four prioritizing questions listed in this chapter. Reflect on each question as it relates to the personal growth goals you created in chapter 9.

4. Draft specific accountability questions for each of your goals and determine the manner and frequency with which you want to be questioned.

ELEVEN

Keeping Score

Appraising the Progress of Personal Growth

I am told that my personality as a child was sometimes rather abrasive. I liked games where the score was kept, and I liked to win. I like to think I was merely competitive; others have said I was argumentative. A running joke in our family is that my dad found me one day a few miles outside of town arguing with a sign. When he pulled up to get me, he asked what I was doing. I told him, "This sign says it's five miles to town, but I know it's only four."

Now that I am all grown up, I'd like to think my competitive spirit works to my advantage without chafing those around me. Friends tell me that I'm generally easy to get along with, but I still have a desire to excel. I now play games just for the fun of it—but of course, I do have more fun when I win!

Appraising the progress of a personal growth plan is a lot like keeping score. It asks the question, How will I know that I am successful? This component of personal growth brings the process full circle. A good growth plan begins with assessment and ends with evaluation. The assessment identifies possible areas for personal growth and the appraisal determines how effective your action plan was at producing growth in those areas. There is little benefit in pursuing growth if you cannot measure the results.

Appraising the growth process has several benefits. First, it helps create momentum for future growth. When you document the cause-and-effect relationship between your personal growth plan and your improvement in a specific area, you gain motivation. Nothing breeds success quite like success. One byproduct of narrowing your D/A Differential is an increased desire to keep growing. That momentum adds leverage to your growth because with it, you can overcome much bigger obstacles than without it. A relatively small object can keep a motionless train from starting to move, but that same object would be totally demolished if it came in contact with a moving train. When you fail to measure your growth, you don't take advantage of the momentum you have already created.

Second, appraising your progress will suggest modifications to your action plan that will make it more effective. If you determine that you have not realized certain goals in your growth plan, you can further examine the process itself to determine how to improve it.

A few years ago I appraised my progress toward the goals in my plan, and it became clear that I had not achieved all I had hoped for in one area. As I asked other questions of this goal, I discovered that I had not placed enough emphasis on accountability partnerships in my plan. The problem was not that I needed more information or experience; it was that I needed more consistent follow through. I included the same goal in my next growth cycle but added an accountability component. The results were dramatically different.

Third, appraisal identifies personal growth patterns. If you persist with personal growth planning over time, you will begin to see your life from a broader perspective, which will lead to more effective evaluation. For example, after a few years of personal growth planning, I realized that I had great difficulty achieving personal and family-life growth goals that appeared in the Responsibility portion of my personal assessment. Because I had a natural tendency to focus on goals that related to other life domains, I consistently struggled to see progress in those two areas. Recognizing the pattern enabled me to ask higher-level questions about my priorities. In this case, consistent appraisal over time revealed a problem with misaligned values. Addressing the underlying issue has enabled me to make much better progress in personal and family life growth.

Appraisal is the critical fourth step in the process of pursuing intentional growth. It becomes the mile marker on the journey to realizing your dreams.

FOUR LEVELS OF EVALUATION

Corporations spend millions of dollars each year sending their people to various training events. Understandably, they want to see a favorable cost/benefit ratio for this investment. They want to be sure that the training is worth what it costs the company. Professionals have done a good deal of research in the area of evaluating training programs to measure their effectiveness. Since personal growth planning is essentially an individual training program, you can benefit from the results of that research. In his book *Evaluating Training Programs,* Donald L. Kirkpatrick identifies four levels of appraisal or evaluation of the effectiveness of a training program.[1]

Reaction

The first level of evaluation is *reaction.* This is the response of the participants during the training and their formal evaluation after it is over. Your reaction to your personal growth plan is important as well. If you do not feel good about the process or do not like the approach, it will be difficult to sustain. The approach to personal growth planning that I've outlined here is very systematic and biased toward highly analytical thinkers. I know from experience that people of all temperaments can use and benefit from this approach, but I understand that some people may need to modify it to fit their way of doing things. How you react to the process is important.

Learning

The second level of evaluation is *learning*: the extent to which participants change attitudes, improve knowledge, and develop skills. You have a distinct advantage in evaluating your own learning because you are better positioned to appraise changes in your attitude or increases in your knowledge or skills.

Behavior

The third level of evaluation is *behavior*. This evaluation measures how effectively attitudes, knowledge, and skills are transferred into real-life situations. Many variables affect the measurement of behavior. For example, trainees may really enjoy a workshop (reaction) and gain practical information that improves a specific skill set (learning). But if they believe that using this newly refined skill will take more time than they have available or will create tension with their boss, they may not actually use the skill on the job. In personal growth planning, most of these variables are under your control. Level three evaluation cuts to the heart of the matter, asking how you have personally changed as a result of the training. Once again, you are in the best position to answer that question.

Results

The fourth level of evaluation is *results*. This evaluation measures how the change in behavior has affected the organization's ability to fulfill its mission. Even changed behavior is not a guarantee of good results.

For example, suppose that you listed a growth goal to develop your leadership skills by reading leadership books during a growth cycle. Let's assume that you had a good reaction to this process—you liked most of the books and enjoyed the process of meeting with your accountability partner to discuss them. Let's assume also that you learned from it—you gained new ideas and leadership principles. Because you were excited about these new principles, you readily tried to apply them to leadership situations—you experienced a change in behavior. Now it's time for level four evaluation: to determine the results of this growth activity on your influence as a leader. Were you actually more effective in leading people? Did your leadership produce positive results in your organization? Were those within your sphere of influence more productive? Did you get the results you were hoping for?

Level one evaluation asks whether you *liked* your growth activity. Level two asks what you *learned* from it. Level three asks whether you *lived* it out. Level four asks if you were able to *leverage* what you learned to obtain the results you desired. All four levels of evaluation are important; each one builds upon the last. As you appraise the results of your growth plan, you will need to evaluate your activities at each of these four levels.

FIVE KINDS OF APPRAISALS

Kirkpatrick's four levels of evaluation provide categories for an appraisal, but you'll need a method of appraisal as well. It will be helpful to appraise the progress of your personal growth plans in one or more of the following ways. There is some overlap between these five approaches and Kirkpatrick's four levels, and taken together, they make a comprehensive approach to measuring the effectiveness of your personal growth plan.

Statistical Appraisal

A statistical appraisal is simply a tally of the components of the action plan. It will reveal whether or not you followed the growth plan as it was mapped out. You determined to read twelve books: how many did you read? You said you were going to go on a date with your spouse twenty-six times: how many dates did you have?

The statistical appraisal is not an absolute measure of the success or failure of your plan. Not meeting the numerical goals that you set does not necessarily mean that you failed. Reading twelve books was not an end in itself; it was attached to some specific growth goal. It is conceivable that you realized your underlying objective without hitting the exact statistical target.

In the same way, dating your spouse is really about growing your marriage. Spending twenty-six evenings together does not necessarily bring a husband and wife closer together. It's possible to hit your statistical goal and still miss your growth objective. In the words of Albert Einstein, "Not everything that counts can be counted, and not everything that can be counted counts." We might consider statistical appraisal to be a level zero evaluation, fitting beneath the threshold of Kirkpatrick's four levels, because it focuses on *participation*.

Motivational Appraisal

A motivational appraisal moves beyond participation to the attitude behind it. It asks if your heart was really engaged in the growth process or if you were merely going through the motions in order to check items off the list. Trust me, when it comes to improving your marriage, your spouse will know if you are simply trying to complete an agenda rather than following the passion of your heart! If you are constantly distracted during your time together and take work-related calls during your evenings out, your spouse will question your progress toward the goal of improving your marriage regardless of whether you check off all the dates on your plan.

You may find it odd that anyone would go through the motions of personal growth planning without engaging his or her heart and soul in the process. But as the deadlines of your growth cycle loom closer, it is quite tempting to race through a growth activity in order to "get it over with" without fully engaging in the process. Perhaps you've read several pages of a book only to realize that you have no idea what you just read. Do you then take a stretch break and reread those pages to ensure your grasp of the material? If you are like me, the answer is sometimes yes and sometimes no. In the same way, you can find yourself putting the wraps on an action plan only to realize that you really didn't benefit from it. A motivational appraisal pushes you to look at each of your growth goals from this perspective and ask, Did I "get it" or just "get it done"?

Practical Appraisal

A practical appraisal combines levels two and three—learning and behavior—of Kirkpatrick's model. It evaluates the increase of knowledge or skill and its impact upon behavior. This appraisal asks, Do I understand it better and can I do it more effectively? One way to evaluate your progress at this practical level is to ask where you are on the four stages of a mastery continuum.

Stage One: Unconsciously Incompetent. When you don't know that you don't know something, you are unable to grow in that area. Therefore, the first barrier to personal growth is ignorance of need. Outside assessment is useful for appraising at this level. Others can flag areas of potential development you may not have considered. If you have developed a personal growth goal in a specific area, you are, by definition, beyond this stage of the mastery continuum.

Stage Two: Consciously Incompetent. When you recognize that you are in over your head in a certain skill area, you have tremendous motivation for personal growth. That is why the Capacity Index, especially the D/A Differential, is such a powerful tool for appraisal. Conscious incompetence—knowing what you do not know—is a healthy and necessary first step toward personal growth.

Stage Three: Consciously Competent. At this level of competence, you can perform the various functions of a given task, but you must prepare thoroughly and think carefully in order to do so. You can perform it predictably, but not as a second nature. The more you know about the subject, the more you realize how much you don't know. This level of competence can become the enemy of personal growth and serve as a barrier, holding your actual capacity much further below your dream than you want it to be.

Stage Four: Unconsciously Competent. True mastery comes when you so fully develop your skill or knowledge base that you can function at very high levels without being preoccupied with the component parts of the process. Ironically, it is at this level that significant growth actually becomes possible. The achievement of this mastery and the unlimited potential for growth beyond it is a powerful reason why you should give priority to building on your strengths. Appraising your action plan at the practical level should include a careful analysis of the things you have learned to do naturally—breaking each one into its component parts. That will enable you to identify transferable principles that can be taught to others. Teaching others can play an important role in your own growth and is what makes multiplication possible, as we'll see in section three.

Strategic Appraisal

Statistical, motivational, and practical appraisals measure the impact of personal growth activities on you as an individual. A strategic appraisal measures the results of your growth on the lives of others and on the organizations of which you are a part. Personal growth begins with you but always moves beyond you to the people and structures around you. Suppose, for example, that you set a goal to become a better parent. Some of your growth activities might be measurable by a statistical or practical appraisal. But you need a strategic appraisal to measure the bottom-line result in the context of your family. What impact has your growth had on the lives of your children? Similarly, you cannot evaluate your growth as a leader apart from your relationship with followers or the organization in which your leadership plays out. A strategic appraisal asks how your growth activities have affected the lives of those around you.

Lifestyle Appraisal

A lifestyle appraisal evaluates the staying power of your personal growth. One of the characteristics of a healthy growth plan, as identified in chapter 6, is that it will be both time bound and habit forming. Although your growth plan operates within the framework of a growth cycle, you will want to incorporate many of its components into your lifestyle and continue them long after the current plan comes to a close. This appraisal will not relate to every single goal, but it will help you evaluate how well your growth activities did at producing life change.

For several years I struggled to cultivate a consistent pattern of personal fitness activities. A lifestyle appraisal helped me realize that if I did not incorporate this goal, with accountability, into my upcoming cycles, I would probably lose whatever progress I'd made in the previous year. Lately I am encouraged to see that as I wind down each growth cycle, I have settled into a fitness routine that I can honestly say is part of my lifestyle, not just part of one year's growth plan.

PERSONAL GROWTH SUMMARY SHEETS

Throughout this book, I have emphasized the importance of putting your growth plan in writing. While there are many ways to do that, perhaps the simplest is to create a Personal Growth Summary Sheet that integrates the components of each growth goal into a single document. This will be an indispensable tool for appraising your growth plan because it contains the details of each goal, including the learning activities associate with it. There are four components to the Personal Growth Summary Sheet. (See a sample in the Appendix.)

Growth Area

First, the summary sheet lists the specific growth area in which you have identified a need for improvement based on your assessment. After you have done a personal growth assessment and prioritized the growth areas you want to include in your plan, write each growth area on a summary and note the part of the assessment process from which it emerged. I do this as though I were recording the path of a file on my computer, using a slash as a separator. So if I decided to work on the leadership skill of change management, I would write this on my summary sheet: Identity/Acquired Skills/Change Management. Identity is the assessment category, Acquired Skills is the sub-component of the Identity Profile, and Change Management is the specific skill I want to develop. If the growth area were parenting, I would document it on my Growth Summary Sheet as Responsibility/Family Life/Parenting. This helps me see at a glance not only the goal but also the portion of my assessment process that generated it. That reinforces the value of the five categories.

Growth Goal

Second, the summary sheet records the growth goal itself in the form of an affirmation statement, a specific description of the outcome you are striving for. If change management is the desired skill, the statement might look something like this: "I am becoming an expert in change management with the ability to anticipate unintended consequences and communicate effectively with the affected people to maximize positive results for the group."

Growth Activities

Third, the summary sheet lists the specific combination of growth assets (experiences, people, and resources) that will facilitate growth in the stated area. Again, if the growth goal is change management, the growth activities might read something like this: "I will study Kurt Lewin's Force Field Analysis model of change dynamics, documenting the restraining and driving forces of a situation before taking action. I will pursue a historical mentoring relationship with Winston Churchill and identify change-management lessons, especially as they relate to communication. I will interview two leaders in my network (Bill and Frank) to learn from their experience in managing recent major changes."

Growth Partners

Fourth, the summary sheet lists the specific accountability formats that you will use to keep yourself focused on the growth goal. A sample statement, based on the change management growth goal might look like this:

I will utilize one-to-one accountability by asking Bob, my supervisor at work, to e-mail me by June 30 to ask about the selection of my Churchill resources. I will ask Bob to contact me in the last 30 days of my growth cycle to schedule a lunch meeting in which I will give him a written report of the change-management lessons I've learned from Churchill. Bob will ask me the following questions:

- Which Churchill resources were most helpful to you in this process and why?

- What was Churchill's most significant change-management experience? How did he handle it, and what did you learn from him?

- Looking back over change management situations you've experienced, in which of them would you have benefited most from

Churchill's example? How might the situation have turned out differently if you had had the benefit of his example?

I will ask my colleague Dave to hold me accountable for interviewing Bill and Frank by September 30. Dave will include these questions in his e-mail to me:

- Did you interview both Bill and Frank?

- What is the most important principle about change management you learned from them?

- How can you apply what you have learned to a current change situation?

I will maintain a change management folder in which I will keep information about Lewin's model and my notes regarding driving and restraining forces for each major change situation. I will have Dave ask to review my folder randomly (at least three times during this growth cycle) to ensure that I'm following through.

Growth Appraisal

Finally, the summary sheet includes your plan for a growth appraisal, stating the time frame and evaluation process you will use to measure your progress toward the growth goal. Your appraisal statement might read something like this:

I expect this growth goal to extend over the entire year of my growth cycle. I will evaluate my progress against the follow-through of my action plan along with a careful review of my affirmation statement in connection with real change situations I encounter this year. I will show my affirmation statement to people in my group who have been affected by changes I have led and solicit their feedback.

A personal growth coach can powerfully accelerate the process of writing good affirmation statements and developing sound action plans and accountability frameworks, especially in your first few growth cycles. To learn more about personal growth coaching, visit www.KeepGrowingInc.com.

You should not consider your growth plan complete for a given cycle until you have developed comprehensive summary sheets for each goal. Bring your first draft of these summary sheets to your closure/kickoff event and gain input from a second source before contacting your accountability partners. When they are finalized, keep your Growth Summary Sheets in an accessible location such as a folder on your desk or your PDA.

THE QUESTION OF OVERKILL

As you review the four steps toward leveraging the power of growth and begin to draft Personal Growth Summary Sheets, you probably feel overwhelmed. It may appear that this is the developmental equivalent of swatting a fly with a bazooka. Why would anyone go through a program as detailed as this?

Your dreams are at stake; that's why.

About an hour down Interstate 25 from my house is the Olympic Training Center in Colorado Springs. It is a state-of-the-art facility, bustling with activity in preparation for the next cycle of Olympic Games. It is not uncommon for athletes at the center to get up at 4:00 a.m. to begin their rigorous training. They work carefully with trainers and dieticians to ensure that their bodies will be as close to peak condition as possible during the Olympic competition. Why do they do it? Because of the power of their dreams.

What makes their dreams nobler than yours? Why would rigorous training be admirable for them but not for you?

There is no more powerful and long-lasting source of motivation for personal growth than your life dreams. Undoubtedly, you will need to adapt this growth model to fit your needs. So do it. But don't sell your dreams short. Look once more at your October Sky, the place where your dream intersects with your Capacity Index. Gaze up to where you want to be, and let that vision refuel your passion to pursue your God-inspired dreams.

LEVERAGE POINTS

1. Analyze each of your goals for these two important factors:

    Timing. Can it be completed in one shot or will it stretch over months, perhaps even the whole year? How will you schedule your activity, by day, by quarter, or other?

    Appraisal. How will you know if you have hit the mark?

2. Integrate all the components of each goal using a Personal Growth Summary Sheet. (Refer to sample in the Appendix.)

3. How might using the summary sheet format create a common framework and language for your interaction with colleagues or those you are mentoring in personal growth?

PART 3

The Power of Multiplying

Multiply the power of your dreams by helping others grow.

Investing in others increases your potential. As they grow, they will help you realize your dream.

Dreaming Times Ten

Cultivating Personal Growth in Relationships

Think back over your formal education. Who was your favorite teacher? What was it about him or her that made learning so enjoyable? One of my favorites was a college professor we affectionately referred to as Dr. K. This prof was always well prepared, and he was passionate about the material for every class session. He employed a variety of teaching techniques, using charts, graphs, and other visual media whenever possible. In spite of the fact that students knew his classes would be challenging, everyone wanted to take them; Dr. K's courses were always full.

You could probably make a similar list of the characteristics of teachers who positively influenced you. But I suggest that beneath the variety of traits and methods that characterize good teaching is a fundamental value held in common by all effective teachers: they feel a responsibility for causing students to learn.

Teaching at this level calls for a paradigm shift that is illustrated by two questions.[1] The old paradigm approaches teaching by asking, What do I want to say about this topic? The focus is on imparting information. The new paradigm asks, What will it take for students to learn? The focus is on effective communication. The first approach places the responsibility for learning on students: if they are motivated, they will learn. The second approach places the responsibility on teachers: if they are motivated, they will teach. But there is a catch: a teacher hasn't taught if a student hasn't learned. If you have ever been privileged to sit under a new-paradigm teacher, you know there is a world of difference between these two approaches.

Now that you understand what it takes to grow and reach your dreams, I issue this challenge: become a teacher as well as a student. Become a person who not only grows to realize his or her dreams but also motivates others to do the same. I challenge you to become a teaching magnet in the school of life, someone whose "classes" are always filled with students eager to be stimulated, eager to learn, and eager to grow.

Why should you do this? What's your motivation to invest your energy in teaching others? At the risk of sounding repetitive, I'll say it once again: your dreams are at stake. In order to realize your greatest God-inspired dreams, you will need the help and support of others. No dream worthy of your best effort can be achieved alone. As you share your dream with others, you will need to help them grow, too, to realize their life-dreams as well as your own. As you leverage the power of your relational network, you will multiply the force of your dream.

INSPIRING GROWTH IN OTHERS

It has been said that all the world is a stage, and that's true, but it is also a classroom. Opportunities to teach and to learn fill every day. The natural flow of life is actually more conducive to learning than many formal training settings for several reasons. If you are to create a learning environment for yourself and those around you, you must capitalize on the learning opportunities that surround you every day. Here's why it makes sense to enroll as a student in the school of life.

First, good learning tends to be social. Formal educational settings often foster a competitive environment among isolated individuals, but the school of life is collaborative, fostering a learning community. Most adult learning programs are intentional about recreating the social component of the school of life by encouraging (or even requiring) study groups. Even when we learn individually through reading or independent study, we generally seek to share what we have learned with others or apply it in the context of our relationships.

Second, school-of-life learning is experiential. The desire to learn is diminished when students cannot readily see how new skills or information apply to real life. People intuitively ask themselves "Why do I need to know this?" or "How will this help me in the future?" In the school of life, we gravitate toward learning opportunities that can readily be connected to life situations. And since self-directed learning is more likely to be applied immediately, it accelerates development by providing real-time feedback.

Third, school-of-life learning takes place on a flexible schedule. Teachable moments do not have to be created; they can be captured. Life happens. And as it does, windows of opportunity to learn open at every turn—if we will only see them. In the words of leadership guru Warren Bennis, learning opportunities "exist in real time, everywhere and all the time. Boring meetings. Unspoken grievances. Closed doors. Unexplained actions. Undeployed talents. Subtle rejections. . . . We're talking about the mundane, the quotidian problems of everyday life."[2] A single moment of reflection energized by the question, What can I learn from this? can transform any life circumstance into an opportunity to grow.

Fourth, the school of life offers the widest course selection. General electives are everywhere, waiting to be "elected." From casual hobbies to life passions, we have a wide selection of majors from which to chose. Even the "required courses" of life, those challenging circumstances that shape character and refine self-awareness, can be supplemented by a recommended reading list of our own choosing.

When you begin to see your relational network as a virtual learning community you will leverage the power of growth not only in your own life but also in the lives of others. You will multiply the power of your dream. Life itself is the most suitable environment for teaching and learning. Take advantage of it. Here are five practical steps for becoming an academic dean in the school of life.

Model Growth

First, intentionally model personal growth values and behaviors. This can be done in two ways, actively and passively. Passive modeling takes place when people observe your attitudes or behaviors but are left to themselves to discern your underlying motives. Passive modeling is a snapshot of growth behavior, but it has no caption. Intentional modeling gives both a picture of the attitude or behavior and some commentary to go with it.

Imagine, for example, that you are on a business trip and have an hour between flights. You are traveling with a colleague from the office. After checking in, you reach for a book in your briefcase, dig out your pen, and begin reading, making notes in the margin as you move down the page. Your colleague asks if the book is any good; you reply with a simple yes and keep reading. That is passive modeling. Your coworker has observed your behavior but has no details to inform what he has seen.

Now picture the same scene, only this time as you pull the book out of your bag, you hold it up for your friend to see.

"Have you read this?" you ask.

"No," he says.

You continue: "Well, in my current growth cycle, I'm working on leadership skills. This is one of the books I'll be reading. By the way, what's the best book you've read lately? I'm always looking for good ideas."

Your friend names the title of a book, then asks, "What was that you said about a growth cycle?"

Now you have an opportunity to provide some detail. "It's just a way for me to be intentional about my personal development rather than settling for whatever happens. Hang on a second while I grab my folder." You pull your personal growth folder out of your bag and remove the summary sheet for your leadership goal. "Here's what I have planned for the leadership part of this growth cycle. Take a look at it if you're interested."

That is intentional modeling. Trust me; it makes a difference.

You might be concerned that talking about your growth goals would seem arrogant, but humility and intentional modeling are not mutually exclusive. In fact, when I enlist accountability partnerships to help me stay on track with a particular growth goal, I include accountability partners who I believe will benefit from exposure to growth planning. That way, they help to keep me accountable for working on my needs, and I have an opportunity to intentionally model growth planing for them.

Opportunities for intentional modeling are everywhere. Imagine attending a conference that has dozens of workshops in addition to plenary sessions. As you sit with a few friends during the first break, they start discussing which workshops to attend. You pull out your PDA, open up the electronic version of your Growth Summary Sheets, and compare them with the list of workshops in the conference brochure. In the background, you hear your friends talking about which sessions "look interesting." You emphasize your desire to be strategic about learning by reviewing your growth goals to see if any workshops relate to them. That exchange will undoubtedly offer an opportunity for intentional modeling. You are humble (admitting your need to grow in certain areas) and intentional (modeling the growth process for others) at the same time. Whether they realize it or not, your friends have just enrolled with you in the school of life. You have created a climate for growth in your relationships.

Remove Barriers

The second thing you must do to create a climate for growth is actively remove the barriers to personal growth. In chapter 4 we considered the barriers to personal growth and realized that there are always restraining forces at work—forces that hold the A on your Capacity Index in place. If there were not, you would be growing all the time. But you aren't. Neither are the people around you. It takes planned activity to consistently decrease your D/A Differential.

One of the barriers you can help remove is the fear of failure. Growth rarely flourishes in a high-risk environment. Create a climate for growth in your relational network, especially your family, by encouraging others to experiment with new skills without being encumbered by the question, What if I fail? Turn failure experiences into detours instead of dead-ends. Talk openly about how you are learning from your mistakes, making them stepping-stones to new horizons. Look for restraining forces in the lives of people around you and take the initiative to reduce them.

Provide Opportunities

Third, create a learning environment for those around you by consistently providing opportunities for growth. Engage the people around you enough to discover their passions, then stimulate their learning with books, articles, and experiences that fit their Identity Profile. Pass along audio teaching CDs. Encourage people to come with you to conferences. Start personal growth groups.

Every few years I take the initiative to start a learning group built around a book that appeals to several people I know. I carefully invite four or five of them to join me in reading one chapter before each meeting. We rotate the responsibility for leading a discussion based on the following questions:

- What statement, principle, or idea in this chapter do I agree with most?

- What statement, principle, or idea in this chapter do I disagree with most? Why?

- What statement, principle, or idea in this chapter do I want to learn more about? How will I do that?

- What is the most practical principle or idea from this chapter for me right now, and how will I apply it?

I emphasize at the outset that anyone who does not read the assigned chapter attends the group that week as a listener only and cannot enter into the conversation. That way, the dialogue doesn't get bogged down with uninformed questions. These discussion groups have been a practical way not only to benefit from the input of others but also to incorporate group accountability into my growth planning.

Create Incentives

The fourth step to fostering a learning environment is to carefully create incentives for personal growth. Some parents pay their children for doing household chores, such as taking out the trash or cleaning their rooms. I suggest that you might pay your children to read books, listen to teaching CDs, or otherwise engage in activities that stimulate growth. I have a standing offer to pay my children $100 if they read the entire Bible in the year after they turn twelve.

When I read books, I mark ideas, quotes, illustrations, and facts, noting the page numbers inside the front cover of the book. I pay my teenage daughter to type these quotes into an electronic document for me so I can file them in my illustration folder. This not only helps me but also enables her to interact with the best content in every book I read.

In an organization you can create an incentive for growth by giving employees one paid day off per year for personal growth planning. You might require them to meet with their supervisor before and after to discuss their growth goals and to provide accountability. You might also consider providing training on personal growth planning for your staff.

Be careful to communicate that you value others independent of their personal growth. People have intrinsic value regardless of how much they grow. When people fail to grow toward their potential, it does not diminish their value but does reduce the chance of fulfilling their God-inspired dreams.

Inspire Dreamers

Fifth, to create an environment for learning, consistently inspire dreams in the people around you. You are reading this book because you want to use the power of your dreams to fuel personal growth. Inspire that same desire in others. Affirm their latent potential. Encourage increased self-awareness. If you want to help people grow, help them dream.

This is a very simple list of ideas for cultivating a climate for growth in your relational network. It is the simplicity of these steps that makes the process so powerful. Anyone can apply these practical steps with dramatic results—including you. But you must take action. We have a dangerous tendency to substitute good intentions for practical action in this area. We settle for thinking about inspiring growth in others rather than actually doing it. I challenge you to become a teacher as well as a learner. Begin to ask the question, What will it take for others to learn? And you will multiply the power of your dreams.

INTENSIFYING THE CLIMATE FOR GROWTH

These five practical ideas for cultivating growth in your relationships can be readily applied to the widest relational network, and you should be generous in doing so. Two facts, however, must be observed. First, some people will be more responsive to your efforts than others. Second, you have a limited amount of time to invest in developing the people around you. Since that is true, you must find the most efficient means of determining who really wants to grow and is open to your help. In mentoring terminology, that is known as *screening in*.

When screening in, the goal is not to keep people out but to let the right people in. It is proactive inclusiveness. For mentoring or coaching to be effective, three things must occur: attraction, responsiveness, and accountability.[3] The mentee must be attracted to the mentor, responsive to his or her input, and willing to be held accountable at an appropriate level. The challenge for mentors is to efficiently determine which prospective mentees fit these criteria.

The best way to screen mentees is to provide practical opportunities for them to demonstrate high levels of initiative. Let's recall the interaction that we imagined between you and a coworker at an airport. You were reading a leadership book as part of your personal growth plan, and you intentionally modeled that action for your coworker. Now suppose you have boarded the plane and your friend continues the discussion of your Personal Growth Summary Sheet, asking how he can create his own personal growth plan. You affirm his interest and say that if he contacts you back at the office, you will loan him your copy of *The Dream Cycle,* from which you learned how to grow on purpose. You offer to help him develop a growth plan *if* he reads the book and completes a personal assessment.

You have just screened in your first mentee. If your friend accepts the challenge, reads the book, and completes a personal assessment, he will have confirmed his motivation to learn by demonstrating a higher level of commitment. Place that colleague on your personal growth hot list: he is worthy of your focused time and effort. Maximize your relationship by intensifying the climate for personal growth.

You'll need to become adept at screening in if you are to intensify a climate for growth for selected individuals. Good screening activities combine two basic factors. First, they should be *autotelic.* That term is derived from two Greek words, *auto,* which means self, and *telos,* which means goal. Autotelic activities are those having intrinsic value; they are worth doing for their own sake. If you attempt to screen in learning candidates with what they perceive to be meaningless activities, they will resent your actions. Nobody likes busywork. Asking your colleague to review your Growth Summary Sheet, read *The Dream Cycle*, and perform a self-assessment are all autotelic activities: they have stand-alone value.

Second, screening-in activities should fit the maturity level of the candidate. When you screen in people, create speed bumps, not roadblocks. Your goal is to draw their desire to the surface by forcing them to direct energy into the learning process, not to squelch their motivation with difficult tasks. Good screening-in activities are both autotelic and reasonable.

All dream-inspired learners cultivate a climate for growth in those around in them. Remember, you cannot reach your God-inspired dreams alone. You must create a team of dreamers who share your vision and are willing to help you achieve it. Cultivate a climate for growth in everyone around you. Intensify that climate in selected individuals, and you will multiply the power of your dreams.

LEVERAGE POINTS

1. Think of the most important relationships in your life domains of family, vocation, Kingdom, and community. List ten key people in each domain. How effectively are you modeling personal growth for these people? To what extent is your modeling intentional?

2. What growth opportunities could you provide for the most important people on the list you've just made?

3. Make a second list, a hot list of people in whom you wish to intensify the desire to grow. How will you screen in these people?

4. Which of your personal growth goals might be shared with a group of people in your relational network? Whom might you invite to participate in a personal growth group? What format would that group take?

THIRTEEN

Dreaming Times One Hundred

Cultivating Personal Growth in Organizations

"It pays the bills."

That weary phrase describes the way many people feel about their employment. When people utter that statement, they are really saying that their job is not very fulfilling, but it provides financial survival—at least for now. Many factors affect the sense of satisfaction a person may derive from work. One of the most important is the feeling that one's work is connected to some important cause. All people want to make a difference in the world by adding value to others. A meaningless job can lead to madness, literally.

In 1944 Allied aircraft bombed a factory operated by Jewish prisoners in Hungary. The next day the prisoners assembled around the ruins of the factory and obeyed their instructions to haul the debris to the other side of the compound. They assumed that the Germans would force them to rebuild the factory. On the following day, the Jewish prisoners followed orders to move the same debris back to where it had originally been. They were surprised, but figured that the Germans either had made a mistake or changed their minds about the location of the rebuilt facility. But it was no mistake. Day after day these prisoners, who were barely surviving under the wretched conditions of their captivity, were turned into "human rats," unwitting participants in a mental-health experiment to see how people respond to meaningless work.

Over a matter of weeks, the prisoners slowly went mad. Some ran into the barbed wire fences that surrounded the compound and were electrocuted; others were shot by guards while trying to escape. The Russian novelist Dostoevsky was right when he said that if you want to utterly crush a man, give him work of a completely senseless and irrational nature. Human beings crave meaning, especially in connection with their work.

Since that is true, two questions are of vital importance for leaders. First, is the presence of a value-added cause the only ingredient necessary to create a climate of growth in an organization? The answer is a clear no. Working for an international relief organization may be rewarding from the perspective of ultimate values but terribly dull from a developmental perspective.

The second question is this: is it possible to create a climate for growth in an organization whose mission is at the lower end of the value-added continuum? In some organizations, the daily activities are dull or routine and it is difficult to see how they add value to the lives of others. The more the purpose of the work has to be explained, the more meaningless the explanation becomes. In that situation, leadership with a developmental bias is even more important.

In short, organizations need to have not only a meaningful purpose to fulfill but also a climate of growth in which to fulfill it. People thrive when they are part of a developmental culture that makes their work meaningful. When people believe that their employer is committed to helping them grow and when on-the-job experiences are part of a learning process, their sense of fulfillment skyrockets.

That brings us to a second aspect of creating a climate for growth in those around us: creating a climate for growth in corporate settings. When you create a learning environment for those with whom you share a common vision, goals, and economic framework, you multiply your dreams at a new level. You leverage the power of growth in your organization.

LEADING WITH A DEVELOPMENTAL BIAS

The first step toward creating a climate for growth in your organization is to adopt a developmental bias. Leaders who have a developmental bias influence their organizations to care for, train, and develop their staff.[1] These leaders help staff members find meaning in their work by creating an environment where learning takes place.

The lowest level of developmental activity in an organization is *staff care*. Although there is a cost for staff care in the form of employee benefits, it is in the best interest of the organization to ensure that its workers are cared for at this basic level. The organization benefits also by creating a pleasant work environment where relationships are healthy.

The second level of developmental activity is *staff training*. Most organizations initiate training to improve the job-related competencies of their employees. These training opportunities usually focus on teams, departments, or positions within the organization that share specific skills.

Developmental Bias Priorities

Developmentally Biased Organizations Give Priority and Focus to ...		
Staff Care	**Staff Training**	**Staff Development**
Health care, social and relational support, spiritual care	Skill training, seminars and conferences; targeted to teams, departments, or positions with common needs	Holistic, less programmatic, dealing with individual growth plans and developmental activities
Primarily driven by the mutual needs of the individual and organization	Primarily driven by felt needs within the organization	Primarily driven by unique needs of the individual

Generalized Issues ◄·· *Customized Issues* ►

The third and highest level of activity in a developmentally biased organization is *staff development*. Staff development has an individual focus. Its goal is to meet the unique needs of staff members based on personal growth goals or the desire for customized training. Very few organizations attend to this level of personalized growth. Some leaders fear that if they invest in their team at the staff development level, they will lose good people to other organizations. But which is worse, developing people only to see them move on, or having underdeveloped employees remain in place?

Developmentally biased organizations believe that part of their purpose is to help each employee discover and fulfill his or her life purpose. These organizations know it is in their best interest to place staff members in the roles that closely match their talents, skills, gifts, and passions. When a staff member's development indicates the need for a new role (based on passion, gifts, and skills), leaders with a developmental bias find a proper fit within the organization or facilitate a supportive transition to a new organization.

Developmentally biased leaders hold two important principles in tension. First, they remember that the organization is the number-one stakeholder. Second, they remember that their employees are more important than the tasks they perform.

The needs of individual employees cannot supersede the purpose of the organization or it will under-perform in the short term and cease to exist in the long term. Neither of these options benefits the employee. Effective leaders understand that they must give their first priority to ensuring that the organization fulfills its purpose or it will disappear. The need for staff development is no rationalization for driving the company into the ground.

Nevertheless, developmentally biased leaders believe their employees are ultimately more important than the tasks they perform. These leaders do not consistently sacrifice staff development on the altar of efficiency. They operate from an abundance paradigm, believing that the release of a staff member to a new role inside or outside the organization may create stress in the short term but will build greater loyalty and support from other team-mates who see developmentally biased leadership in action.

Adopting a developmental bias fosters a climate for growth in your organization. When you believe that the development of your coworkers and employees is important not only for their well-being but also for realizing your shared goals, you will leverage the power of growth in your organization and multiply the power of your dreams.

THE INTEGRATED MODEL

The second step toward creating a climate for growth in your organization is to integrate the desire for growth in every aspect of the organization. Dr. Shelley Trebesch has created an integrated model for personal development based on her doctoral research on OMF International (formerly China

Inland Mission), the mission agency founded by J. Hudson Taylor. For the purposes of her research, Dr. Trebesch defined development as "the individual and corporate processes God uses to grow individuals into who they have been created to be, and lead and empower them to fulfill their unique destinies . . . while participating in the overall mission of the organization."[2] Trebesch has identified six factors that affect the development of individuals within a Christian organizational context. I believe her model applies also to corporations. Although marketplace leaders may need to make slight modifications in Trebesch's schematic, the process as a whole is transferable.

- *Faith Assumptions.* Is the organization undergirded by biblical and theological truths that affirm God's desire to actively shape and develop people toward their full potential?

- *Values.* Does the organization have a core of implicit beliefs that reinforce the priority of people and their primacy as an organizational asset?

- *Organizational Dynamics.* Do the organizational culture, structure and systems work together to enhance a developmental bias? Do individuals who are pursuing personal development feel they are going "against the current" or forced to circumvent systems and structures?

- *Experiences.* Can individuals readily identify a wide range of developmental experiences (events or situations) that have been intentionally prepared and delivered as part of an organizational design?

- *Leaders.* Do leaders at all levels in the organization model personal development, purposely come along side others to assess areas for growth, and seek to connect developing leaders with new opportunities for service?

- *Individuals.* Do individuals in the organization have a learning posture, a healthy measure of self-awareness, and a sense of expectancy about future development?

In an integrated organization, developmental assumptions and values frame the organization's culture, structures, and systems. Individuals have a responsibility for their own growth and must be willing to take advantage of experiences provided for them by leaders. When an organization makes the desire for personal growth a part of its culture, the development of each member is multiplied.

THE CREATION OF FLOW

Integrating personal growth into the culture of an organization leads to the creation of *flow*. Flow is an academic term that describes the balanced convergence of challenge and skill, opportunity and capacity.[3] If we face an opportunity in which the challenge is much greater than our skill, we become anxious. Conversely, if our skills are much higher than the challenge, we become bored, even apathetic. But a balance between skill and challenge creates flow. Think about playing the piano. Learning scales and playing a simple song like "Mary had a Little Lamb" challenge the skills of a beginner. But once basic skills are in place, the player becomes bored if more challenging songs are not included in the lesson.

When a person experiences flow, he or she focuses on a clear goal with a high level of concentration. Her sense of time is altered, and the person may notice the clock and say, "Have I been working on this for three hours? It seems like only ten minutes!" Although people who experience flow are not self-focused, they emerge from it with a higher level of self-esteem; they feel good about themselves. People commonly express the idea of experiencing flow as being "in the zone."

Personal growth is essentially the creation of self-directed flow experiences. Growth is an upward spiral of matching increased capacity with more challenging opportunities. Developmentally biased leaders and organizations foster the creation of flow for workers on the job whenever possible. They encourage workers to create personal growth plans that generate flow experiences beyond the scope of the working environment. When employees associate flow, on or off the job, with the values and training provided by their employer, a sense of engagement, loyalty, and productivity tends to increase.

There seems to be an intuitive sense within employees that work should produce personal satisfaction. Surveys suggest that as many as 80 percent of adults claim they would continue to work even if they did not need the money to survive.[4] Yet most of these same people find themselves staring at the clock every day in anticipation of quitting time. Although we want to find value, meaning, and flow at work, far too many of us live for the weekend. This tension creates a wonderful opportunity for developmentally biased leaders. If you are successful in creating flow within your organization, you will multiply the power of your dreams exponentially.

EMBEDDING DEVELOPMENTAL VALUES

It has been stated that "it is impossible to create an environment that will foster flow without commitment from top management. Leadership must embrace the idea that before products, profit, and market share, they are primarily responsible for the emotional well-being of their workers."[5] In both the corporate and nonprofit sectors, leadership is the ultimate variable in creating a climate for growth. One-shot growth opportunities will never do. Employees readily discern the dissonance between a program of the month and the organization's underlying values. Disingenuous attempts at creating a climate for growth may actually be worse than doing nothing at all. To create a genuine climate for growth, you must embed the concept of personal growth into the value system of the organization. Four key words will help you navigate this process: model, measure, manage, and motivate. Let's look at each one briefly.

Model

First, you will need to model personal growth for your team. Organizational culture flows from the behavior of high-level leaders. In the day-to-day working environment, the actions of leaders always trump policy manuals in defining "how we do things around here," the basic expression of organizational culture.

Most high-level leaders are committed to personal growth. But there is a difference between growing as a leader and modeling growth for others. You must find ways to talk about your growth plan, share what you are learning, and become transparent about your own creation of flow. Don't assume that people will notice your increased capacity and associate it with a commitment to personal growth.

Measure

Second, demonstrate the importance of personal growth by measuring it along with other organizational performance indicators. Workers intuitively discern the relative importance of new initiatives by how often and how seriously leaders measure them. If you follow training in personal growth planning with a requirement to submit personal growth goals, you demonstrate the value associated with the behavior. Including personal growth items in the staff meeting agenda and providing a way to attach growth goals to annual performance reviews will reinforce the corporate value of personal development.

A word of caution is called for here. Measuring personal growth activities requires a high-trust environment. If workers view this process as one more way to document their under-performance, it will not result in a climate of growth. Consider implementing this model in phases, beginning with higher-level managers and then widening it to include the entire team. Emphasize your underlying desire to help each worker grow toward his or her full potential. The best way to start is by providing training on personal growth planning followed by coaching for those who are highly motivated.[6]

Manage

Third, manage with developmental objectives. Recognize the priority of matching team members' skills with organizational challenges as a means of creating flow. Demonstrate flexibility with teams, allowing individuals to be temporarily reassigned to another role or even transferred to another department when it becomes obvious that their personal development will be enhanced by the new responsibilities. Balance the tension between the organization as the primary stakeholder and the individual's value beyond his or her performance.

Motivate

Fourth, motivate the team based on developmental objectives. Offer incentives to individuals and teams that demonstrate a practical commitment to personal growth. Push them to connect the dots between their personal growth goals and organizational effectiveness. Then reward them openly when they hit the mark. Consider adding a personal growth or flow award to your annual review procedure.

DEVELOPMENTAL BIAS IN ACTION

Practically speaking, what does this developmental activity look like in real life? In addition to my leadership at Keep Growing Inc., I have been privileged to help shape the developmental bias of Top Flight Leadership, a nonprofit organization focused on developing young leaders. Using Dr. Trebesch's factors as the backdrop, here is a practical snapshot of developmental bias in action.

First, Top Flight has articulated faith assumptions that provide a foundation for its commitment to develop others. These include the following:

- Everyone has the capacity for God-inspired dreams that will shape their unique destiny.

- Everyone can increase his or her capacity by growing on purpose. We will be held accountable to God for how we have used our giftedness.

- God develops leaders over a lifetime. How we respond to God's shaping influence affects the timetable for our development and calls for a lifelong perspective.

- The most important role of leaders is to develop other leaders.

These assumptions compel Top Flight to create developmental opportunities for the team.

A developmental bias has been intentionally embedded within Top Flight's culture by means of core values that emphasize the value of people: "Top Flight Leadership gives priority to the personal growth of our staff, leaders who engage in our training experiences, and those who benefit from our products." This organization believes the development of staff members will result in increasing loyalty and motivation to pursue the vision and mission of the organization. If staff members grow out of their role with Top Flight Leadership or discover that their passions no longer overlap sufficiently with the corporate vision, leaders graciously release them to pursue their destiny elsewhere. The manner in which past employees speak about Top Flight's culture will become a valuable recruiting tool for those who replace them.

Top Flight has been intentional about communicating the essence of the organizational culture it is trying to create. They have done that by making explicit statements to new staff members in the opening section of their staff manual. Several of these statements exhibit a developmental bias, but one makes it explicit:

Make personal growth a continuing priority. Never become complacent with where you are now; always strive to become more of what God intended you to be. Enthusiastically pursue the personal growth planning process that flows from Top Flight Leadership's staff-development systems. Find a personal accountability partner. Read books. Talk with humility about what you are learning. Pass along growth assets to other members of the team (articles, books, tapes). Cultivate a technology edge. In short, *keep growing.*

One of Top Flight's ultimate contribution statements also speaks directly to this issue: "A lasting legacy of Top Flight Leadership will be a model organizational culture that balances the pursuit of aggressive growth with the intentional personal development of every team member."

I recently advised Top Flight's leaders in the creation of an annual customized personal growth plan for every staff member. Personal growth planning is a standing agenda item for all staff meetings at this organization, and detailed reporting of personal growth goals is made during biannual strategic planning sessions. There is a practical commitment to include personal growth expense lines in the budget. Top Flight invests 10 percent of general revenue in others with the aim of advancing the personal growth of young leaders around the world based on applications received from its web site. All of these steps represent an intentional effort to embed a developmental bias into the organizational culture, systems, and structures.

Clearly, it is possible to create a climate for growth in an organization. But is that something you can do?

Picture yourself at a coffee shop, sitting in a soft and comfortable wingback chair. One leg hangs comfortably over the arm of the chair while the other is propped on a table. Some of your coworkers are lounging nearby. Soft background music sets a pleasant mood for discussion as you sip your favorite Starbucks coffee and scan the printout of your personal growth goals.

As you sit together in this casual but serious atmosphere, each team member shares how he or she has grown over the past year. The conversation is free-flowing with questions and comments coming from all sides of the circle. Now and then you pause to celebrate the progress of a team member and how that personal growth has helped the organization. There is a sense of safety and vulnerability. No one feels the pressure to pretend or present a false impression of his or her progress. In fact, when a teammate says, "This goal was a complete bust," his honesty is rewarded by caring questions motivated by a genuine desire to help him grow. There is a growing sense of expectancy in the dialogue as momentum builds for next year's growth plans. All members of the team genuinely believe that God will continue to shape them, superintending their development, and that the relationships, systems, structures, and culture of the organization will offer the practical support they need.

Does this sound too good to be true?

I have just described my most recent meeting with members of Top Flight Leadership, which was part of a structured weekend of personal growth and strategic planning activities. What they have done, you can do too. It is possible to create this same kind of atmosphere in your organization.

KEEP GROWING

If you are a leader, I challenge you to move beyond a commitment to your own growth and develop a bias for the growth of those in your organization. It's the right thing to do. And, pragmatically speaking, it's the most efficient thing to do. If you do not foster a growth environment, you will struggle to attract and keep valuable staff members.

If you are not an organizational leader, I challenge you to take responsibility for creating personal flow regardless of the bias of the culture in which you work. Austrian psychologist Victor Frankl wrote that you cannot attain happiness by wanting to be happy. It comes as the byproduct of working for a goal that is greater than yourself.[7] Tap into your God-inspired dreams; make a commitment to decrease your D/A Differential. Capitalize on the places where this journey overlaps with your workplace. Find ways to balance increased challenge with increased capacity and thereby create flow. Remember, your boss is not ultimately responsible for realizing your dreams—you are. And as you create an atmosphere of growth in your organization, you will multiply the power of your dreams.

LEVERAGE POINTS

1. To what extent do you lead with a developmental bias? What specific activities would you cite to make your case? Are these activities mostly related to staff care, training, or development?

2. Review the six factors in Dr. Trebesch's integrated model. Rank these in descending order based on your evaluation of how well they are developed within your organization. What evidence would you provide if asked to justify your assessment? Consider taking a survey of your staff to validate your conclusions.

3. When was the last time you experienced flow at work? How often do those who work for you experience flow? What does this say, if anything, about how your job fits into your personal development?

4. Which of the four basic methods for embedding value into the fabric of an organizational culture do you do best? What areas do you most need to improve?

5. How might you connect personal growth planning with performance reviews in your organization? How do you think your team would react to that?

Afterword

The Ultimate Legacy: Cultivating a Field of Dreams

What will be your legacy? What reality will you leave behind when you are gone? That ultimate contribution will be framed largely by your life-dreams. Your achievements will be the framework for your legacy. Hidden behind that frame, however, is another potentially larger contribution that will dwarf even your grandest vision of your realized dream. Project yourself into the future and imagine not just what *you* will accomplish but what *others* will accomplish because of you. This is your legacy once removed, the field of dreams that you have planted in the lives of others.

Your work will accelerate the closing of the D/A Differential of those around you. Your role in their lives, though once removed, will be obvious. In other cases, your contribution will be unnoticed. But the hidden component of your legacy consists of adding value to others, not in being recognized for doing so. Helping others realize their dreams is an autotelic endeavor: it carries its own reward. Someday God will tell "the rest of the story," letting you know all that has resulted from the seed you have sown into the lives of others.

I know the reality of what I'm sharing with you from personal experience. And I'll give you my final charge with an example from my own journey. When I started college to study radiologic technology, I reconnected with my faith roots and started listening for God-inspired dreams for the first time in years. I came home from college one weekend to participate in a conference hosted by the church in which my dad served as pastor. On a Sunday afternoon, I had the privilege, along with my parents, of having lunch with the weekend's speaker.

As we talked over lunch, the speaker took an interest in me. He engaged my questions and sharpened my thinking. As our time together came to a close, I was anxious about getting back on the road for the four-hour drive back to school. After saying goodbye to my parents, I walked out to the driveway and got in my car. As I started to back out, I looked up and saw our guest walking toward me. As I rolled down my window, he leaned over to look me in the eye and offer a few words of encouragement. He affirmed my potential, told me that God had big things in store for my life, and said a very simple prayer, asking for a blessing on my journey—not just the drive but throughout my life. His remarks were simple and took only a moment to deliver, but I remember them vividly.

Why? Because they became a seedling in my field of dreams.

The speaker for that conference, the guest who spoke words of encouragement about my dreams, was John Maxwell. At that time, John had yet to write a leadership book, and the idea of investing in other leaders through megaleadership conferences was still a distant dream. He was working on his own D/A Differential, and as he did, I watched from a distance. I doubt that I am the only one who could point to a seedling planted by John in 1982—a seedling that has grown to become part of his hidden legacy. In the two decades that have followed, he has influenced an untold number of people to dream and to grow. By doing so, he has multiplied the power of his own dreams a thousandfold.

So here is my closing word to you: Do something more with your life than chase your own dreams. As worthwhile as they are, your own dreams do not scratch the surface of what God has in store for you. Plant dreams in the lives of others. Spend your life cultivating not one but a field of dreams, leaving behind a hidden legacy that will powerfully shape the world for years to come.

Appendix
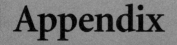

Sample Personal Growth Summary Sheet

Jeff Johnson   March 15, 2004

1. **Growth Area:** A specific area for improvement based on the assessment process.

   Identity/Acquired Skills/Change Management

2. **Growth Goal:** A specific description of the end result I am striving for in the form of an affirmation statement.

   I am becoming an expert in change management with the ability to anticipate unintended consequences and communicate effectively with the affected people to maximize positive results for the group.

3. **Growth Plan:** The specific combination of growth assets (experiences, people, and resources) that will facilitate growth in this area.

   I will study Kurt Lewin's Force Field Analysis model of change dynamics, documenting the restraining and driving forces of a situation before taking action. I will pursue a historical mentoring relationship with Winston Churchill and identify change-management lessons, especially as they relate to communication. I will interview two leaders in my network (Bill and Frank) to learn from their experience in managing recent major changes.

4. **Growth Partners:** The specific people and accountability formats that I plan to use to keep me focused on this goal.

I will utilize one-to-one accountability by asking Bob, my supervisor at work, to e-mail me by June 30 to ask about the selection of my Churchill resources. I will ask Bob to contact me in the last thirty days of my growth cycle to schedule a lunch meeting in which I will give him a written report of the change-management lessons I've learned from Churchill. Bob will ask me the following questions:

- *Which Churchill resources were most helpful to you in this process and why?*

- *What was Churchill's most significant change-management experience? How did he handle it, and what did you learn from him?*

- *Looking back over change management situations you've experienced, in which of them would you have benefited most from Churchill's example? How might the situation have turned out differently if you had had the benefit of his example?*

I will ask my colleague Dave to hold me accountable for interviewing Bill and Frank by September 30. Dave will include these questions in his e-mail to me:

- *Did you interview both Bill and Frank?*

- *What is the most important principle about change management you learned from them?*

- *How can you apply what you have learned to a current change situation?*

I will maintain a change management folder in which I will keep information about Lewin's model and my notes regarding driving and restraining forces for each major change situation. I will have Dave ask to review my folder randomly (at least three times during this growth cycle) to ensure that I'm following through.

5. **Growth Appraisal**. My plan for the time frame and evaluation process I will use to measure my progress toward the growth goal.

I expect this growth goal to extend over the entire year of my growth cycle. I will evaluate my progress against the follow-through of my action plan along with a careful review of my affirmation statement in connection with real change situations I encounter this year. I will show my affirmation statement to people in my group who have been affected by changes I have led and solicit their feedback.

Notes

Chapter 1: Personal Capacity

1. Mihaly Csikszentmihalyi, *Good Business* (New York: Viking Press, 2003), 78.

Chapter 2: The Dream Cycle

1. 1 Samuel 3:1.

2. 1 Samuel 3:5.

3. 1 Samuel 3:9.

Chapter 3: Beneath the Surface

1. See Daniel Goleman, Richard E. Boyatzis, and Annie McKee, *Primal Leadership: Realizing the Power of Emotional Intelligence* (Boston: Harvard Business School Press, 2002), 111–112. In his model of self-directed learning, Boyatzis describes the difference between one's ideal and real self as exposing strengths and gaps. I have substituted the word "needs" in place of "gaps" so readers unfamiliar with the original source can more easily follow my ideas. Boyatzis' model actually includes five discoveries; I have only highlighted the first three. The remaining discoveries are experimenting with and practicing new behaviors, thoughts, and feelings to the point of mastery, and developing supportive and trusting relationships that make change possible.

2. You can read Joseph's story in Genesis 37–50.

3. Moses' story is found in Exodus 2.

4. J. Robert Clinton, *Leadership Perspectives* (Altadena, Calif.: Barnabas Publishers, 1993), 86–89.

Chapter 4: Change Dynamics

1. Leonard Sweet, SoulTsunami (Grand Rapids, Mich.: Zondervan, 1999), 73.

2. Lewin's force field model for evaluating change has been widely referenced in leadership literature. I first encountered it in J. Robert Clinton's book, *Bridging Strategies* (Altadena, Calif.: Barnabas Publishers, 1992).

3. George E. Valliant, *Adaptation to Life* (Cambridge, Mass.: Harvard University Press, 1995), 120.

4. See Galatians 6:7.

5. Philippians 1:6 (The Message).

Chapter 5: The Dream Team

1. Isaiah 54:2–3 (KJV).

2. Norman Grubb, *C. T. Studd: Cricketeer to Pioneer* (Fort Washington, Pa: Christian Literature Crusade, 1982), 120–121.

3. Sword of the Lord Publishers, "D. L. Moody," http://www.swordofthelord .com/biographies/moody.htm.

4. Lyle W. Dorsett, *A Passion For Souls* (Chicago: Moody Press, 1997), 81.

5. Ibid., 393.

6. Ibid., 394.

7. Ed Reese, "The Life and Ministry of James Hudson Taylor," Wholesome Words, http://www.wholesomewords.org/missions/biotaylor2.html.

8. The lessons highlighted here are summarized from: Roger Steer, *J. Hudson Taylor* (Littleton, Colo.: OMF Books, 1993), 175–176.

9. C. Howard Hopkins, *John R. Mott, A Biography* (Grand Rapids, Mich.: William B. Eerdmans Publishing Co., 1905), 19.

10. Ibid., 91.

11. Ibid., 223.

Chapter 6: Focusing Your Energy

1. Proverbs 19:2.

2. I believe God gives special abilities, described in the Bible as spiritual gifts, to those who follow Him. While there is room for disagreement among Christians about how spiritual gifts operate, all agree on this point: every Christ-follower has at least one gift, and it should be used to serve others. See 1 Peter 4:10.

3. Marcus Buckingham and Donald Clifton, *Now, Discover Your Strengths* (New York: Free Press, 2001), 126. *Now, Discover Your Strengths* is not a religious book, and the authors readily acknowledge that talents may be viewed as gifts from God, or accidents of birth. I believe God is the creative force behind the miracle of life.

4. Ibid., 47.

5. I first discovered the life domains in Tom Patterson, *Living the Life You Were Meant to Live* (Nashville, Tenn.: Thomas Nelson Publishers 1998), 86.

6. Warren G. Bennis and Robert J. Thomas. *Geeks & Geezers: How Era, Values and Defining Moments Shape Leaders* (Boston: Harvard Business School Press, 2002), 47.

7. See Luke 19 and Matthew 25.

Chapter 7: Generating Momentum

1. I am indebted to the teaching of John Maxwell for the redefinition of charisma

as a focus on others, by way of a video clip included with a mentoring kit, *Lead On.* "Discussion Starter Video," *Lead On*, VHS, ed. Richard R. Wynn (Englewood, Colo.: Emerging Young Leaders, 1998).

2. Proverbs 27:17.

Chapter 8: Taking Inventory

1. I am indebted, in part, for the idea of self-awareness as a subset of emotional intelligence to Daniel Goleman, Annie McKee, and Richard E. Boyatzis, *Primal Leadership: Realizing the Power of Emotional Intelligence* (Boston: Harvard Business School Press, 2002).

2. I first encountered these subcategories in J. Robert Clinton, *The Mentor Handbook* (Altadena, Calif.: Barnabas Publishers, 1991), pp. 4-4 through 4-27. I have modified the labels.

3. Exodus 33:15.

4. Exodus 33:11.

5. See the book, *Please Understand Me: Character and Temperament Types*, David Keirsey and Marilyn Bates (Prometheus Nemesis Book Company, 1984). The DiSC Personal Profile is available online at www.resourcesunlimited.com.

6. Purchase of the book *Now, Discover Your Strengths* by Marcus Buckingham and Donald Clifton (New York: Free Press, 2001) includes a one-time, online assessment that will identify your top five Signature Themes of talent.

7. A downloadable spiritual gifts assessment tool is available at https://www.gospelcom.net/topflight/resources.

8. For information on personal coaching in the area of destiny awareness and the creation of a personal mission statement, visit http://www.KeepGrowingInc .com.

9. 1 Corinthians 9:24–27 (The Message).

Chapter 9: A Bridge to Your Dreams

1. John C. Maxwell, *The Success Journey* (Nashville, Tenn.: Thomas Nelson, 1997), 49.

2. Martin Gilbert, *Churchill: A Life* (New York: Henry Holt and Company, 1991), 110–120.

3. Proverbs 3:34.

4. Steven Covey, *The 7 Habits of Highly Effective People* (New York: Simon and Schuster, 1990), 134.

5. Dr. and Mrs. Howard Taylor, *Biography of James Hudson Taylor* (London: Hodder and Stoughton, 1965), 27.

6. For more on learning from historical mentors, see chapter 13 of my book *Leadership Insights for Emerging Leaders and Those Investing in Them*, available from Top Flight Leadership at http://www.topflight.org.

7. For more information on enlisting a personal growth coach, visit http://www.KeepGrowingInc.com.

Chapter 10: A Cord of Three Strands

1. George Barna, *The Second Coming of the Church* (Waco, Tex.: Word Publishing, 1998), 19.

2. Ecclesiastes 4:9–12.

3. In their book, *Accountability: Becoming a Person of Integrity* (Indianapolis: Wesleyan Publishing House, 1991), Wayne Schmidt and Yvonne Prowant use this scripture as the source for citing specific benefits of accountability. I have modified their ideas in this section.

Chapter 11: Keeping Score

1. Donald L. Kirkpatrick, *Evaluating Training Programs,* (San Francisco: Berrett-Koehler, 1998).

Chapter 12: Dreaming Times Ten

1. I first heard these two questions from my friend and mentor Keith Drury, a new-paradigm professor at Indiana Wesleyan University.

2. Warren G. Bennis and Robert J. Thomas, *Geeks & Geezers: How Era, Values, and Defining Moments Shape Leaders* (Boston: Harvard Business School Press, 2002), 179.

3. My view of the mentoring process has been significantly shaped by J. Robert Clinton and Paul Stanley, *Connecting: The Mentoring Relationships You Need to Succeed in Life* (Colorado Springs: NavPress, 1992).

Chapter 13: Dreaming Times One Hundred

1. I first heard these three expressions of a developmental bias from Dr. J. Robert Clinton, professor of leadership at Fuller Theological Seminary.

2. Dr. Trebesch's dissertation, *The Development of Persons in Christian Organizations,* is available on CD-ROM and may be requested by e-mail at SGTrebesch@aol.com.

3. I've summarized these ideas about flow from the writing of Mihaly Csikszentmihalyi, specifically from his book, *Good Business* (New York: Viking Press, 2003).

4. Ibid., 86.

5. Ibid., 113.

6. Keep Growing Inc. specializes in providing personal growth training and coaching as well as consulting for leaders on how create a developmental culture. Visit http://www.KeepGrowingInc.com for more information.

7. Csikszentmihalyi, *Good Business*, 56.